UNIVERSITY OF
WOLVERHAMPTON

Harrison Learning Centre
Wolverhampton Campus
University of Wolverhampton
St Peter's Square
Wolverhampton WV1 1RH
Wolverhampton (01902) 322305

B T Batsford Ltd • London

First published 1995

Typeset by Lasertext Ltd, Stretford, Manchester
and printed in Great Britain by Butler & Tanner, Frome

Published by
B.T. Batsford Ltd
4 Fitzhardinge Street, London W1H 0AH

A CIP catalogue record for this book is available from the British Library

ISBN 0 7134 7548 X

This book is dedicated to W. M. de Majo, Founder President of the International
Council of Graphic Design Associations (ICOGRADA) whose enthusiasm for the
field inspired generations of designers and students.

Contents

Acknowledgements

4

I would like to thank Gabriela Wadham-Smith for her patience in typing up the final manuscript and my husband Dr Walter Eric Boettcher, for his advice and encouragement throughout this project. My thanks also to the Commissioning Editor, Richard Reynolds, for his unflagging support. Acknowledgement should also go to Martina Stansbie, Assistant Editor, whose timely contribution to the project was invaluable. Special appreciation goes to students and colleagues at Ravensbourne College of Design and Communication, London who supported my proposals for and implementation of a programme of study in graphic design history and theory. And finally, I would like to acknowledge all the contributors for their co-operation and encouragement in realizing the publication of this book.

Every effort has been made to trace the copyright holders of illustrations used in this book. The publishers will be happy to rectify any omissions in subsequent editions. The editor and publishers would like to thank the following for permission to reproduce illustrations: pp 26, 28, 30 Imperial War Museum, London; p 38 from the collection of Lee Young; pp 34, 37, 40 author's collection; p 57 John Bushnell; p 56 Susan Costanzo; p 93 © The Board of Trustees of the V&A; pp 89, 91, 96 London Transport Museum; pp 99, 100, 101 courtesy of the artist and Galerie Lelong, New York. Thanks also to the other sources, acknowledged in the captions.

Notes on the Contributors

John Bushnell is Professor of History at Northwestern University. He has written numerous articles on Russian and Soviet history and is author of *Moscow Graffiti: Language and Subculture.*

Joanna Close was until recently Senior Lecturer in the School of Art, Architecture and Design at the University of Humberside, where she taught Graphic Design, Illustration and Theoretical Studies. Her current research interests include the 'designer decade' (the 1980s) and image making in the Labour Party.

David Cook is a freelance writer and art critic who has written extensively on male gender, popular culture and graphic design. He is editor of the forth-coming book *Men and Shopping*, to be published by Lawrence and Wishart, and is currently putting together books on men's magazines and computer games.

Michèle-Anne Dauppe is Senior Lecturer in Historical and Theoretical Studies at the School of Art, Design and Media, University of Portsmouth. She is a contributor to design journals such as *Eye* and *Form und Zweck.*

Diane J. Gromala studies the relationships among design, technology and various subcultures including cyberpunk and the Solidarity movement in Poland. She is a frequent lecturer at international art and technology conferences and recently completed a two year residency in the Virtual Environments project at the Banff Centre for the Arts in Canada. Professor Gromala is Director of the New Media Research Laboratory at the University of Washington in Seattle.

Steven Heller is the editor of the AIGA *Journal of Graphic Design* and author of over 30 books including, *The Savage Mirror: The Art of Contemporary Caricature, Borrowed Design: The Use and Abuse of Historical Form, Italian Art Deco: Graphic Design Between the Wars* and *Dutch Modern: Graphic Design from DeStijl to Deco.*

Victor Margolin is Associate Professor of Design History at the University of Illinois, Chicago. He is an editor of *Design Issues* and the author or editor of several books including *American Poster Renaissance, Propaganda: The Art of Persuasion* and *Design Discourse: History, Theory, Criticism.*

Kevin Robins works at the Centre for Urban and Regional Development Studies, University of Newcastle upon Tyne. He is currently doing research on new communications technologies and urban development. He is co-author of *The Technical Fix* (1989) and co-editor of *Cyborg Worlds: The Military Information Society* (1989).

Notes on the Contributors

David Rowsell is Lecturer in Graphic Design History and Theory at Ravensbourne College of Design and Communication, London. His current research interests concern issues of communication and aesthetics within graphic design.

Edward Triggs is Senior Lecturer on the Design Faculty of the University of Texas at Austin, where he teaches Communication Design and Persuasive Design.

Teal Triggs is Course Leader for the School of Graphic Design at Ravensbourne College of Design and Communication, London and a Design Historian with specific interest in graphic design history and theory. She received an MA in Art History from the University of Texas at Austin in 1983 and in 1990 an MA in Design History from Middlesex Polytechnic. Her writings have appeared in a number of books as well as in design publications including *Eye* and the *Journal of Design History*. Currently, she is working on a study of fanzine culture in Britain.

John A. Walker, BA ALA, studied Fine Art at university in Newcastle upon Tyne, then came to London in the early 1960s and worked in the civil service and in libraries. At present, he lectures on Art and Design History at Middlesex University. He is the author of several books and many articles on contemporary art and mass media, photography and design historiography.

Geoff Warren studied typography at the London College of Printing and was awarded an MA in Design History from Middlesex Polytechnic in 1990. He is a vicar in Watford and has lectured part time in Cultural Studies at Central St Martins, London. Currently he is researching for a PhD on the Ideal Home Exhibition at Middlesex University.

Krzysztof Wodiczko is a public artist and designer known for his public projections on city monuments (since 1980) and his design interventions, such as the Vehicle (1972), Homeless Vehicle (1988), Poliscar (1991) and recently the Alien Staff: a performative electronic instrument designed for contemporary immigrants to help them come to terms with their changing identities and to communicate the history of their experience. He is Director of the Center for Advanced Visual Studies at Massachusetts Institute of Technology in Cambridge, Mass., and teaches at the Ecole Nationale Supérieure des Beaux-Arts in Paris. Retrospective exhibitions of his work accompanied by catalogues were held in 1992 at Fundaçio Antoni Tapies in Barcelona and at the Walker Art Center in Minneapolis.

Jon Wozencroft worked for printers, publishers and record companies before setting up the audiovisual publishers *Touch* in 1982. For ten years he has collaborated with Neville Brody, with whom he has produced two books for Thames and Hudson. In 1990 they set up *FUSE*, a forum for experimental typography and winner of numerous awards for its approach to digital design. In 1992, he published the magazine *Vagabond* with writer Jon Savage. Wozencroft is main tutor in Interactive Multimedia at the Royal College of Art.

Introduction

Teal Triggs

Graphic design has left its mark on the contemporary urban landscape. We are bombarded daily with information – music and political posters fly-posted on walls, shop front signage, advertising billboards, medical warnings, newspapers and magazines, transport maps and timetables, television screens and even 'lost animal' messages tacked precariously on telephone poles. The passer-by is confronted by a vernacular culture of design. Messages are continuously being sent, received and decoded while walking down high streets, driving along highways, sitting passively in front of televisions or interacting with the latest computer games. By necessity, graphic design has appropriated a diversity of visual forms and languages so as to convey information, ideas and beliefs to an ever-increasing cross-section of the global community who are ever more accustomed to graphic design conventions.

Over the last ten years, graphic design has increasingly enjoyed a higher profile within both the public domain and the general design community. A succession of exhibitions focusing on graphic design and its practitioners have been held at important cultural institutions such as the Victoria and Albert Museum, Design Museum (London), Walker Art Center, Cooper-Hewitt and the Herb Lubalin Study Center for Design and Typography. Television programmes and the national press, especially in Britain, have featured stories on the work of graphic designers as well as on the history and theory behind design-related issues. Design conferences which examine particular concerns as well as specialized publications such as *Eye*, *Information Design Journal*, *Visible Language* and *Design Issues* have provided equally important forums for academic and professional debate. But despite its visual impact, little attention has been given to how we analyse the process and interpretation of graphic design within broader cultural, social, economic and political frameworks. In addition, the way in which graphic designers might employ the profession's history for critical reflection on their own work has also failed to be addressed sufficiently.

Jorge Frascara, Professor of Art and Design at the University of Alberta, has defined graphic design as

. . . the giving of appropriate form to a communication directed at having an impact on audience attitudes, knowledge, or behavior.[1]

Introduction

From this it is an easy step to propose that graphic design ephemera provide important visual documents of the cultural, environmental, economic, social and political attitudes of any given point in time. For if communication is to be effective, then the graphic object must be articulated clearly; it must engage and be understood by its target audience. Many graphic design programmes in educational institutions remain rooted in art historical practice where information is often presented as chronology, 'hero' biography and anecdotes or organized formally into stylistic art and design movements. These approaches no longer satisfy the demands placed upon students and design professionals who increasingly are required to understand the broader context in which communication operates. Is it enough to study the graphic object from the standpoint of colour, composition, medium or provenance, or should graphic design history consider other elements linked to client perception and intended audience? As the graphic design profession matures, the scope for critical analysis and evaluation of its history and theoretical discourses necessarily broadens. With shifting perceptions, a reappraisal of methodological approaches must take place.

The intent of this book is to provide a variety of ideas and methodologies which may be applied to understanding visual communication. Adoption of one approach does not necessarily negate the validity of another, rather, a combination of approaches might be considered when faced with a specific design task. The essays provide a number of perspectives currently undertaken by academics and design professionals in Europe and North America. The book is not meant to be read from cover to cover, but rather is to be considered a source of ideas and may be read selectively for relevant information, reference or for prompts for further discussion.

The essays cover pragmatic social issues, often discussed in graphic design history. Joanna Close, for instance, examines representations of men and women in wartime venereal disease propaganda and the multiple relationships inherent in the process of design, production and consumption. Similarly, Geoff Warren confronts the issues arising from charity advertising, positioning the discussion within economic and political contexts. David Cook speculates on the problematic relationship between masculinity and consumption in men's magazines.

A second area of emphasis is directed towards cultural issues as they affect the visual nature of design. The graphic languages favoured by the 'designers' of British fanzines, Polish Solidarity posters, American protest campaigns as well as of graffiti found upon the walls of Moscow rely on culturally specific coding systems for their effectiveness. Ideas of rebellion and protest form an underlying agenda for the majority of visual and textual languages adopted by subcultural and counter-cultural groups. Diane J. Gromala and Victor Margolin argue that the production and design of graphic materials plays an important role in the process of political change. Simultaneously, this relationship reflects a state of ongoing interactivity between design, production and mediation. John Bushnell observes how graffiti can be used for staking territorial claims and as a visual symbol of identity, but suggests the eventual breakdown of such explicit messages as a form of cultural opposition.

The concluding sections explore language as concept, the mapping of meanings and resulting visual aesthetics. With the advent of new digital techno-logies, the visual world has been altered, as the actual space in which communication takes place is redefined. Communication output of the 1980s, whether conventionally printed or screen-based, has been subjected to postmodern analysis embracing simulation, pastiche and parody. Kevin Robins examines the nature of post-photo-graphic experience, which rests between the 'real world' and what Baudrillard described as the new world of simulation. In her piece on television graphics, Michèle-Anne Dauppe argues for the establishment of a critical framework for analysing televisual languages. Although technological advances must be taken into account, television and computer-generated images should also be consid-ered within a broader set of historical and cultural determinants. Television pro-vides merely one form of global community. Krzysztof Wodiczko argues for a local community-led future for communication networks in the form of the Poliscar mobile communications and living units for the homeless.

The development of theoretical frameworks in graphic design has centred primarily around the adoption of semiotic analysis – especially the process of transmitting language as coded systems. Jon Wozencroft examines this, while Edward Triggs explores the reception of such persuasive messages. The trans-lation of spatial experience into a series of efficiently decipherable codes is found in John A. Walker's discussion of the London Underground diagram. Steven Heller seeks to contextualize graphic design ideology by raising questions about the relationships of form, function and fashion. This discussion is extended by David Rowsell, who introduces an additional element of 'aesthetic vision'.

But where does all of this lead us in terms of communicating design? Since 1922, when W.A. Dwiggins coined the phrase, 'graphic design', designers have had to adapt to changes in client and audience needs. Equally, they have had to respond to rapidly developing communication technologies. For students and practitioners alike it is essential to recognize both technical and cultural change and their underlying ideologies so as to meet the demands of an ever more ephemeral century.

Media Representations

Redesigning Men: **Arena Magazine, Image and Identity**

David Cook

When interviewed about the launch of British *Esquire*, the men's glossy magazine, Lee Eisenberg commented that 'magazines are the creation of the culture they live in'.[1] Of course, most magazines reflect existing cultural mores and are products of well-established markets. This is hardly surprising as they are costly long-term investments, and the average commercial publisher is not willing to gamble with an untested or risky venture. But occasionally a spark of innovation will pay off; something original is created and comes to life in the form of a magazine.

The brief

The mid–eighties, as we are often reminded, were a boom time for men's consumer markets. The launch of *Arena* coincided with the infamous Levi's 'Launderette' and 'Bath' campaigns, and the rest, as they say, is history. According to this view, *Arena* was created to fill a gap in a pre-existing market and was simply a reflection of changing cultural attitudes. In reality the story doesn't quite read the same way. The advertising revenue was not simply there for the taking, and the content and design of the magazine did not just pander to the moods set by the marketeers or the average 'new man' in the street. In fact, despite the advertisers' much vaunted 'new man' concept, the boom years of 1985–6 and the ascendancy of male-orientated street fashion, the launch of *Arena* was problematic, and in order for the magazine to survive it needed to communicate a new sensibility through fresh ideas and bold design. Indeed, as Dylan Jones (editor 1988–92) explains, *Arena* was very much an experimental project.

I mean *Arena* was done on a wing and a prayer. It could have easily folded after one or two issues. Even Nick Logan was worried about doing a men's magazine that was fashion based…because advertisers would be scared that it was a gay magazine.[2]

This explanation contradicts rhetoric of a 'new man' phenomenon and the idea that there was a ready-made market waiting to be tapped. The Levi's and Brylcream campaigns may indicate foresight on the part of some advertisers, but as Dylan Jones further suggests, most were extremely reluctant to get involved with innovations in the men's market.

Actually advertisers were behind everybody. They were resistant to the style mags, and they were resistant to the men's press. They didn't understand it. They almost wished it wouldn't work.

Advertisers were always behind everybody else. Some say that during the 1980s they were at the cutting edge of culture, they were making the waves. It's absolute rubbish.[3]

Jones' attitude is clearly embittered by his negative experiences of trying to attract advertising revenue when editor, and suggests that *Arena* was not a response to advertisers crying out for a marketing vehicle. For Dylan Jones and Nick Logan, the publisher, it was an uphill battle to produce a magazine that was both innovative and successful. The magazine was built on the ideological and financial success of *The Face* and although it was pitched at a different target audience, men in their early to late twenties, it attempted to syphon off readers who had cut their teeth on the style press. *Arena* was proposed as a commercial venture, but it never attempted to net a mass audience. The magazine was speaking to a particular kind of man who had grown up through Glam Rock, Punk and the New Romantics, and as Jones claims, to a man of a certain age who had become used to seeing images of himself.

[*Arena*] wasn't such a shock to them. Again it was generational, it was aimed at appealing to a very limited number of men. I mean *Arena* sells 90,000. When it was launched it sold about 55,000, and that's a relatively small amount of people.[4]

Accusations from the academic Left that the bulk of commercial magazine publishing reinforces stereotypes and is reluctant to represent progressive change may well be true. Indeed the very notion that all magazines are merely reflections of existing cultural norms helps to reinforce this belief. However, commercial media does not share a common manifesto, rather it allows for individuality and niche products in an increasingly fragmented market-place. In *Arena*'s case, the market-place in general and advertisers in particular were sceptical of the project due to the problematic relationship between masculinity and consumerism. However, *Arena*'s subsequent success illustrates that commercial media, although generally resistant to innovation and radicalism, can be altered and corrupted from within. In this way it is possible to view *Arena* as a fragment of the commercial media playing a pro-active part in the development of gender issues. As Dylan Jones suggests, *Arena* was quite prepared to engage with gender issues, and it did so despite the prejudices of most advertisers.

In many ways you have to bring all the interesting things through the back door; to talk about gender, to talk about sexuality, culture and at the same time aiming specifically at men.[5]

Design as content

Primarily it was the design and fashion photography in *Arena* that addressed issues of male gender and sexuality. The features and essays which dealt with the representation of masculinity followed on later, and as the magazine matured, the relationship between editorial and image became more squarely balanced. Thus the magazine provides an invaluable insight into the relationships between word and image, editorial and advertising, identity and appearance, to both historian and practitioner.

The fashion photography and the graphic layout of the magazine certainly indicate how the consumption of style was made acceptable to some men, despite the tentative relationship that existed between men, fashion and consumerism. Compared to dedicated titles aimed at men which deal with cars or computers, the magazine is unashamedly glossy and design-led. Neville Brody, who as Art Director of *The Face* effected its transformation into 'Britain's Best Dressed Magazine', was employed by Logan to design *Arena*. Brody came up with a magazine that visually referred to *The Face*. He continued to break established typographic rules and explored fresh relationships between typography and image, designing a distinctive and original masthead for the cover. The art direction was not excessively top heavy, rather the design of the magazine was as important as the editorial content. Brody established a coherent design narrative by reinterpreting variations of the helvetica typeface throughout the magazine, and this has created a continuity in the magazine over the years. This design solution rejected the ephemeral eclecticism of *The Face* presumably because *Arena* was pitched at an older target audience, but similarities are evident. As William Owen suggests, in design terms at least, *Arena* was a logical progression.

13

Brody's constant investigations into the possible combinations of magazine type hierarchies yielded some elegant and very practical solutions to the problem of leading the eye around the page. As the editorial [of *The Face*] matured, so did its design, and in many respects this was a magazine that grew up with its readers who, like the art director, then graduated to *Arena*.[6]

If the design of *Arena* was more conservative than that of *The Face*, it was adventurous when compared to other magazines including top women's fashion titles such as *Elle* and *Vogue*. Finally a men's magazine title had been established that in terms of visual stimulation, style and design ignored the assumption that men could not be lured by the romanticism and style of fashion magazines.

The amount of fashion featured in *Arena* also countered the assumption that men were not interested in their self-image. Not since the demise of *Man About Town* in the late 1950s had a non-trade British men's magazine showed such a committed interest in fashion. *Town* magazine in the 1960s showed a mild interest in fashion but it was not treated as an integral part of the magazine. *Arena* was without doubt the first British men's magazine that showed the male as an object in fashion imagery.

[In *Arena*] Pictures of young male models are portrayed in passive, 'feminised' poses, to the camera. The male reader is with a challenge, the new object of his gaze is another man. We are invited to take pleasure from these male bodies and the clothes they wear. There is a sensuality about these images which until now has been completely absent from publications for men.[7]

The style of the fashion photography, like the general design of the magazine, was a slightly toned down interpretation of the way men's fashion had been tackled in

The Face. Accordingly, the styles and images presented in the fashion shoots were eclectic and did not place importance on representing stable identities and fixed gender codes. The fashion pages presented a diverse mix of traditional and radical icons that, like the self-referential discussion of masculinities in the editorial features, raided the historical closet.

Some of the images presented in the fashion pages of *Arena* may seem to represent traditional gender roles, but the magazine never endorsed a simple definition of masculinity. A traditional representation of masculinity could only be read as one style option against a fractured and diverse array of other more challenging masculinities. As a consequence of such a transient and theatrical context, the link between representation and meaning became blurred.

For example, in issue 15, Spring/Summer, 1989 a fashion shoot entitled 'Legion' addresses this blurred relationship between representation and meaning. Shot on location in Aubagne, France, the photographer Michel Haddi used soldiers from the French Foreign Legion as models, wearing clothes ranging from the retail outlet The Duffer and St George to the army surplus shop Laurence Corner. The images in this fashion shoot could have been seen to be reinforcing rigidly conservative gender codes. However, the repressive language of masculinity perpetuated by military institutions is subverted in the context of a fashion magazine. The military metaphor does not repress, it is put up for sale, objectified and turned into a commodity. As such, the images become macho drag in the same way as military styles have been consumed by gay culture. In the late 1980s, straight men also appropriated military fashions; chinos, desert boots and bomber jackets have all entered the vocabulary of menswear. Thus, the military reference need no longer be a conspicuous reinforcement of traditional gender roles, but rather, a meaningless expression of male glamour in the theatrical context of fashion imagery. Again, the relationship between representation and meaning is undermined.

Perhaps if the fashion pages of *Arena* constantly repeated the same images of masculinity, academics would be able to extract some meaning from them. Yet one month the magazine may represent military images or do a fashion shoot in an east London boxing club as in 'Second's Out' (issue 15), whereas another issue may deal more directly with camped-up fashion imagery as in Juergen Teller's 'Candy Coloured Clowns' (issue 9, Spring/Summer, 1988).

Arena also often dealt with openly sexualized images of masculinity, putting the male model in a pose traditionally reserved for women. For example, in 'Debret Pack' (issue 4, Summer, 1987), Michel Haddi presented posed images that would never have been dealt with outside the gay press before the launch of *Arena* to a male consumer audience. In one pose, the model with hand placed down the front of his trousers, bare chested through open jacket, is drawing attention to the flesh that is hidden. In the opposite image, the model with coat hanging off the shoulder is adopting a traditional catwalk pose. In 'Wide Boys Awake' (issue 10, Summer, 1988), images directed by the influential fashion stylist Ray Petri further confront the reader with challenging images of masculinity. Are we to suppose that the two embracing male models are bonded through celebration of their own narcissism, or drawn together by sexual attraction? Either way, this image confronts traditional attitudes towards masculinity.

Fashion photography in *Arena* consistently raids the closet of historical styles, without making any precise ideological reference to those periods. For example, 'Fin de Siècle' (issue 7, Winter, 1987–8) refers to the 1890s but mixes in other historical references. Furthermore, the caption accompanying the fashion spread endorses the visual eclecticism. It reads: 'decadence and formalism; sometime in the not too distant past, somewhere in the heart of Europe, history repeats itself with modernist edge'.[8] The fashion imagery mixes references to the late nineteenth-century dandy with 'new man' imagery. Finally, the image of the model looking in the mirror questions a plethora of certainties. It depicts a man consuming his own image, his own reflection. The viewer does not even see a direct view of the model's face, we too can only consume the image. The image denies all references to actuality and historical context. We cannot find a definition of masculinity in this image because meanings on all levels are blurred, conflicting and hidden.

Many of these images, viewed individually, may seem to hold specific meaning. But, as a body of work, the fashion photography in *Arena* confronts the gaze with a catalogue of eclectic styles with contradicting meanings. It is possible to conclude that *Arena* challenges institutions of masculinity by dealing with a variety of contradictory images, presenting them as a series of stylistic options. This theoretical assertion gains coherence by considering that features in the magazine have stated an awareness of gender issues. As Dylan Jones suggests, there is a tradition of masculinity that *Arena* is trying to reject. He criticizes *GQ* for adhering to codes of masculinity that are an anathema to his own and ostensibly to those of his readers.

I think *GQ* appeals to a certain kind of man, but it's almost the kind of man you hoped didn't exist any more.[9]

Looking at other magazines that are traditionally aimed at men – dealing with cars and sport, and even the men's glossies that have appeared in *Arena*'s wake – an infinitely more limited and constricted view of masculinity is offered. In fact, if you look at the main consumer titles pitched at male audiences you will notice that traditionally men have been actively discouraged from talking about themselves at all. Men, it appears, feel more comfortable busily concerning themselves with inanimate, cold and hard objects – their computers, cars or golf clubs. Anything so long as they are not drawing attention to themselves. Conversely, the type of fashion photography displayed on the pages of *Arena* signifies a triumph of style over utilitarian sensibilities.

Arena was the first of the general interest men's magazines that openly discussed notions of masculinity and by doing so confronted the notion that masculinity is an unquestionable and fixed truth. By looking at design and fashion imagery and demonstrating a willingness to discuss masculinity, *Arena*'s success suggests that for a certain proportion of men, tensions between masculinity,

15

consumerism and puritanism were beginning to be questioned. Significantly, these themes were tackled through the language of typography and fashion photo-essays, as well as by features about sexual politics.

The Face, and more recently *Arena* have certainly contributed to an atmosphere that confronted both the British ambivalence to visual culture and style-led design, and the male phobia of glossy magazines. With *The Face*, Logan helped to establish the roles of the graphic designer and fashion photographer as principal communicators, and this tradition was not lost with the slightly less streetwise *Arena*. This is not to underestimate the written contributions in any magazine. Yet it must be heartening for practitioner and graphic historian alike to see the fluid and expressive qualities of graphic design and fashion photography contributing to complex debates alongside the written word.

'Wide Boys Awake', Martin Brading, Arena, Number 10, Wagadon

Our Image of the Third World

Geoff Warren

National newspapers regularly display advertisements for a variety of charities. This discussion considers some of the issues raised by the advertisements of those concerned with the problems of the Third World. Sometimes these advertisements are produced in response to a particular crisis, sometimes they are part of the regular advertising of the organization. In order to provoke a response, they often work by attempting to portray, through a picture or words, the plight of those in need. However, because they are produced in Britain to be read by people in Britain, they can say as much, if not more, about the ideas, politics and social relations of Britain as they do about the problems of the hungry.

Third World charity advertising developed after the Second World War. Wars produce refugees, orphans and hunger; Oxfam and Christian Aid were founded in response to those problems created by the Second World War and most other charities were founded after then. Because one of the major problems caused by this and subsequent conflicts was the enormous number of homeless refugees, 1959–60 was designated World Refugee Year. It was this Refugee Year and the Congo famine of 1960 that first drew the attention of the public to the need for aid abroad. E. Hereward Phillips, who masterminded the Refugee Year fundraising campaign in Britain, identified both the concern felt by people and their sense of hopelessness at the scale of the problem. What was required, she suggested, was to reach their 'guilt complex'.

Thus, early post-war advertisements are based on a simple analysis of the problem, namely a 'caritative/relief' paradigm of development, combined with an attempt to create guilt in the reader. For example, a 1958 Oxfam advertisement depicting a Korean child with both legs amputated is headed 'Please enable us to rescue…*Helpless Victims of Conflict* '. A decade later, another Oxfam advertisement for the Biafra famine consisted of the headline 'Skin stretched over ribs, enormous heads, pot bellies, wasted buttocks and sticks for arms and legs'. Advertisements like these laid the foundation for the large number of campaigns which, to this day, have continued to show suffering and emaciated people. Pictures of children in particular have been used in order to activate a compassionate response. Consequently, the image of the starving child has long been established as signifying Third World problems.

In order to provoke feelings of guilt or compassion, these advertisements construct a relationship between the recipient of charity and the reader, sometimes contrasting our comfortable and extravagant lifestyle with that of people in

poverty. Such advertisements imply that the helpless victim of poverty and malnutrition could be assisted if only a wealthy individual like the reader would give
some money. One problem with this is that it is an incorrect and damaging representation of people who live in poor countries. Another is that it helps to perpetu-
ate incorrect ideas of why these countries are in economic difficulty, obscuring
the role wealthy nations play in the causes of their problems.

Ideas about the underlying causes of poverty changed as understanding
developed. In 1969, Christian Aid produced an advertisement that showed a picture of a pile of text books accompanied by the heading, 'What Christian Aid
preaches'. Clearly sandwiched between books on pest management, advanced

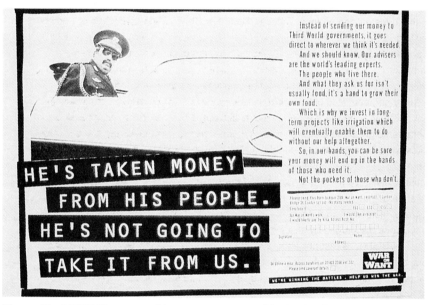

**War on Want 1985. The cropped image suggests wealth, domination and exploitation.
Photographing from below enhances the status of the subject and the pose thus
connotes power. The word 'money' adjacent to the Mercedes symbol reinforces the
suggestion of wealth.**

accounting, trades unions, workshop technology and the fundamentals of modern
agriculture was a book on family planning. This advertisement represented a quite
different analysis of the problems of hunger and how they should be tackled. In
addition to the introduction of birth control, the text books implied education in
modern practices and technology. The initial caritative/relief development paradigm was seen as inadequate and was superseded by one of modernization. Poor
countries were compared with wealthy ones and the differences were explained
by their clearly observable lack of modernity and industrialization. It was thought
that if poorer nations imitated industrialized ones, the wealth created would trickle
down to even the poorest members of the country. Despite a degree of truth in
this view of modernization, changes often exacerbated problems or introduced

new complications. Furthermore, attempts to introduce modern technology and methods often 'foundered on the administrative or political inadequacy derived from the poverty they were meant to cure'.[1]

The two advertisements produced by War on Want reflect a further change in thinking and a quite different understanding of the causes of poverty. Ideas developed, particularly in Latin America, that challenged the modernization paradigm and replaced it with structuralist ones. A whole series of debates and complex analyses focused on the structures of international economic relations and the social structures within countries whereby some were privileged at the expense of others. These models drew attention to the economic imbalance in the exchange of commodities from developing countries with manufactured products of the industrialized nations. They identified how the unequal structures of trading relations kept poorer countries dependent on the wealthy. This approach was further refined by the use of class analysis within the poorer countries. In such countries not all are poor, there will be a wealthy 'centre' with a poor 'periphery'. Keeping large groups of the population marginalized benefitted both foreign industry and domestic elites, for it allowed wages to be kept down and profits up.

The War on Want advertisements illustrated draw on these later development paradigms. The Latin American dictator represents the wealthy and powerful elites within poorer nations, and the 'debt crisis' advertisement is a specific example of the unjust economic relations between rich and poor nations. The way in which these advertisements work is different to those based on the caritative/relief paradigm. These advertisements invite the reader to share in War on Want's outrage. Instead of guilt, they intend to provoke feelings of indignation or anger that can be discharged by alliance with, and donating to, War on Want.

It is obvious that not everyone, and especially not those associated with the four banks indicated in the advertisement, will agree with the views expressed. Indeed, depending on the ideas held by the reader, the outrage provoked may well be against War on Want itself. Normally, marketing people consider charity advertising to be 'direct response' advertising, the main aim of which is to stimulate a response in the reader – usually a donation to the charity or to sign a petition. The underlying presuppositions of the different development paradigms have important implications for this task. The paternalistic benevolence of the caritative/relief and modernization paradigms suggest that change can be brought about by a process that is essentially *harmonious*, because they indicate an outcome where ultimately all will benefit. The later paradigms have an underlying presupposition of conflict – between the poor and those who benefit from the situation as it is. People may be prepared to offer support when the advertisement suggests that they are in a benevolent relationship with the recipient, or where the problem is shown as involving change in the recipient's country. They are less likely to offer support where the message challenges their own lifestyle or reflects critically on the role of their own nation. The problem of communicating such messages is further exacerbated by the very images that have been established by charity advertising as signs of the Third World situation, which have been adopted by the media in general. These have contributed to a public perception that the problem

19

is 'over there' and often due to natural disasters, backwardness and inadequacy of people in poorer countries. There is no indication of unjust and exploitive economic and trading relationships between rich and poor nations.

Despite a widespread understanding that developed within many charities that the problems they were facing were structural and complex, much advertising continued to be based on the caritative/relief paradigm. Following the appalling famine in Ethiopia in 1984–5 and the enormous publicity it received, Oxfam produced a report *Images of Africa*, on the negative consequences of publicity. The report showed that much coverage was based on a mobilization of stereotypes in a simple 'them' and 'us' binary opposition. Those concerned with development

20

War on Want Campaigns Ltd. 1986. This advertisement refers to the debt crisis where initially acceptable loans developed into ones entailing crippling repayments.

education held that the major tasks were to create an awareness of the need for change in wealthy nations, and of the effort, courage and dignity with which people in the poorer nations were grappling with their problems. They wanted charity advertising to be part of this educative process. They argued for *positive* not *negative* images to be used of people in Third World countries and wanted advertisements to address the unjust structural relations between nations. Nevertheless, fundraisers within charities have argued that the task of charity advertising is to raise money by 'direct response'; additional messages, controversial messages, political messages, conceptually challenging messages are all considered to make this harder and reduce the likelihood of a supportive response.

21

(Left) Disasters Emergency Committee 1989. (A group that co-ordinated appeals but that did not necessarily represent the approach of the individual organizations concerned.) The subject, depicted from above, is presented as weak and a passive recipient.

(Right) Christian Aid 'Rights Campaign' 1989. The subject is photographed from below to enhance her stature and dignity, and she is in an active rather that a passive pose. The advertisement is based on the concept of empowerment. The choice of a woman was also deliberate because of particular concerns about the problems of women in poor countries.

These debates have taken place within an increasingly difficult political and economic context in Britain. At the coming to power of Margaret Thatcher in 1979, the aid budget was first drastically cut, and then allowed to decline.[2] Not only did government action and rhetoric serve to undermine concern for the Third World, its economic policies and the rise in unemployment made fundraising more difficult. Furthermore, pressures and shortages experienced by groups like schools and hospitals increased the number of organizations seeking donations. Charities of all kinds found themselves set in a market where they were competing with each other, increasing the pressure upon them to maximize income. This has meant that their advertising messages have had to conform to the relative conservatism of potential donors.

In addition to these problems of the 'charity market' and the conservative ideology of the public, there are further restrictions placed on charity advertising as a force for change. If those actively seeking to help people in poorer countries have come to the view that the most important need is for changes in the policy of Western governments, in trading relations and regulations, in the activities of multinational companies and the exploitive activities of industries like the arms trade, it remains that charities concerned to help people in poorer nations are forbidden by law to campaign for these ends. The Charity Commissioners produced a guidance leaflet which expressly forbade charities from: 'Seeking to influence or remedy those causes of poverty which lie in the social, economic and political structures of countries and communities. Bringing pressure to bear on a government to procure a change in policies… Seeking to eliminate social, economic, political or other injustice'. It is for this reason that Amnesty International cannot operate as a charity. The crucial point of this is that charities receive significant tax benefits as part of their income which they would lose if they lost their charitable status. It has been alleged that right-wing groups and individuals have specifically targeted organizations like Christian Aid, Oxfam and War on Want, making complaints to the Charity Commissioners about their publicity and advertising. War on Want, before its near collapse, attempted to circumvent the problems imposed by charity law by establishing a separate campaigns unit, W.O.W. Campaigns Ltd. However, this was an isolated attempt to break the chain of power relations which exercises control over the public definition of the causes of poverty. The frequently-repeated dependency images of suffering that have been established as signs of the Third World fail to represent the complexity of the problems and mask the role played in them by the wealthy nations. These images, which arose from an earlier understanding of development issues, have been perpetuated by the ideology of potential donors and the way this is determined by the political and economic situation both within this country and in its relations with the Third World.

Venereal Disease Propaganda in the Second World War

Joanna Close

Venereal disease is not a pleasant, popular, or readily popularized subject. It was an important and highly problematic social and political concern of the Second World War and ultimately a threat to the war effort. As is the case with any socio-sexual crisis, such as the AIDS pandemic, the network of relationships within and surrounding it comprises interwoven dynamics of exceeding complexity. Analysis of visual and textual representations of women and men in connection with such crises must take account of traditional and transitional moral attitudes and conditioning in relation to gender, sexual identity and taboos.

Little work has been carried out specifically on wartime venereal disease propaganda. Studies of other aspects of the war are numerous. Those concerned with visual material, such as posters, often confine themselves to examinations of designed products in isolation, with little or no analysis of associated social and cultural relationships which surround their design and production, their consumption and, importantly, everything of any bearing that lies between the two.[1]

To describe, analyse or criticize the colour, form and scale of a poster, including the typeface used, is merely to scratch the surface of design analysis. Similarly, to discuss at length the poster's designer – their life history, lifestyle and personality – encourages esoteric elitism, and is of little consequence when examining a designed object and its significance in wider culture and society. Object or designer-based commentary on design is appropriate within design studios – both in educational institutions, in the form of 'crits', and within client presentations in industry. Such activity should not, however, as is often the case, pose as design historical analysis.

Designed artefacts and their designers do not *in themselves* represent objects of sufficient importance for study or establishing lines of enquiry.[2] All designs have multiple relationships within culture and society; these relationships result in multiple meanings. It is naive to discuss design and design history as one would discuss a piece of design in its narrow studio context. Rather, in order to ensure a thorough reading of any designed object, it is necessary to delve into the complex network of relationships pertaining to it,[3] so as to make *connections*, which facilitate interpretation and understanding of the ubiquitous multiple meanings and innumerable nuances of design.

Let Knowledge Grow

This essay is based on a larger study of British and American propaganda in connection with venereal disease during the Second World War. Wartime public information about venereal disease in Britain was insufficient and inexplicit. Mass-Observation surveys,[4] together with letters to the press, provide evidence of widespread public dissatisfaction with government handling of the problem. When venereal disease showed signs of reaching almost epidemic proportions,[5] a grandiosely entitled official propaganda campaign was launched in the autumn of 1942 – 'Let Knowledge Grow'. This press, poster, radio and film campaign lacked direction and cohesion and combined moralistic scaremongering with an almost total lack of practical information. It can perhaps best be described as too little, too vague and too late.

American servicemen have been blamed consistently (by the general public at that time, and in numerous subsequent British publications concerned with the Second World War) for leading British wartime womanhood astray. In so doing, the servicemen are purported to have played into the hands of enemy propagand-ists. The US troops' 'invasion' of Britain in the spring of 1942 is presented, at best, as having adversely affected the venereal disease issue and, at worst, as being entirely responsible for Britain's post-1942 near-epidemic.[6] When American troops arrived in Britain, attempts by the US Army to contain the problem of venereal   disease were hampered severely by British law. Britain's Venereal Diseases Act of 1916 rendered slanderous any implication by one person that another was infected. A report by the American Social Hygiene Association observed that 'Nothing like the public education carried on in this country [America] has been experienced by the British public'.[7]

People in Britain needed and, on the whole, were ready to welcome such education. Predictably, some found the 'Let Knowledge Grow' campaign's discussion of syphilis and gonorrhoea, in their daily newspaper, difficult to stomach over breakfast. Statements made to Mass-Observation researchers confirm this: 'I think the information distasteful and objectionable'; 'My wife was up in the air about it, as if it was my fault. It's not a nice way at all, and I expect a great number of people will be disgusted about it'.[8] The majority of people, however, felt that the veil of secrecy drawn around venereal disease, by the Government and medical professions, simply added to the trauma of war. The conclusions of a Mass-Observation Survey, carried out shortly after the launch of the 'Let Knowledge Grow' campaign, exhibit the extent of public ignorance at that time:

...many do not even know the name of the disease and it had to be explained that 'pox' or 'clap' were meant. Even then the majority of women had only the haziest notion of what these diseases were; ...Men had a much more profound knowledge of the general social problem, but even they knew little about its prevention. Nobody in the whole sample mentioned anything about symptoms, apart from a few people saying that they had no idea of the symptoms and would not know if they had the disease.[9]

American pressure helped prompt the British Government to launch its 'Let Knowledge Grow' campaign. Similarly, American military influence was instrumental in the establishment of Britain's Defence Regulation 33B (1943). This compelled anyone suspected of having venereal disease to undergo treatment once they had been named by at least two individuals.[10] In 1944, whilst 823 women were reported to Medical Officers of Health in England and Wales, only four men were similarly named.[11] Traditional attitudes of the time laid the blame for the spread of venereal disease unfairly – but none the less squarely – on women.

Don't be a dope with a dose!

A striking comparison can be made between the visual artefacts of Britain's public information campaign, 'Let Knowledge Grow', and examples of American military propaganda concerned with venereal disease, disseminated in Britain at that time.[12] The American propaganda does not warrant the term 'campaign', as it was patently not conceived as a coherent whole. It is none the less consistent in its vivid portrayal of American attitudes to venereal disease and American male attitudes to women. Viewed alongside examples of British military venereal disease propaganda – for example, a 1941 design by Abram Games, official poster designer at the War Office – the two countries' social and cultural differences are brought into sharp relief. Britain's dutiful 'You owe it to…your womenfolk' contrasts starkly with the American's dismissive 'Leave 'em alone'.

The American military material is the complete antithesis of the British approach to venereal disease propaganda. It must be remembered that, except in the case of Games' hygiene poster for the British Army, the markets for this American and British propaganda were very different: the American propaganda was aimed at servicemen, for consumption within a totally male-oriented milieu, whilst Britain's 'Let Knowledge Grow' campaign had a much wider, public information remit. Whereas the British posters are typographically sophisticated and use photographic imagery, sometimes together with collage or stencil and airbrush techniques, American posters concerned with venereal disease are much more amateur in nature, sporting crude and insensitively hand-drawn letterforms in conjunction with imagery that is often less sensitively drawn. Words are also used differently: American copy refers to 'prostitutes' and 'procurable women' rather than the euphemistic 'easy girl-friend' of its British counterpart.[13]

American venereal disease propaganda is routinely derogatory towards women. Frequently, the combined visual/verbal message is essentially that of women's synonymity with the disease. The Americans distributed such propaganda on matchboxes as well as posters. One such matchbox is recollected as bearing a drawing of a woman beside a lampost (signifying prostitution), together with the copy, 'I'll give you something you haven't had before'.[14] Such blatant degradation of women, which is present throughout American venereal disease propaganda, is particularly evident in four posters designed by US Army Private M. Franklyn. One of these bears an image of a smiling, glamorous woman juxtaposed with a red-tailed snake with a red, spitting tongue. The copy alongside the woman reads, 'By comparison a rattlesnake is harmless'. Alongside the snake, the copyline is 'He warns first!', whilst the poster's strapline reads, '"Leave 'em alone" Don't be a dope with a dose!' Another of Franklyn's posters in the same series bears a similar stereotyped image of an alluring woman, with the addition of a facial expression of sultry innocence. The copy reads, 'Beautiful? If you could see what the doctor sees you'd "Leave 'em alone"....'.

A third poster in the series departs from this theme and plays upon men's fears of horrifically painful treatment for venereal disease. The poster bears a black and white image of a sweating man in a hospital bed, in pain and terror, his hair standing on end. At one side of the bed is a trolley laden with bottles and, at the other, a vicious torture-inflicting machine – a robot-like creature with eyes

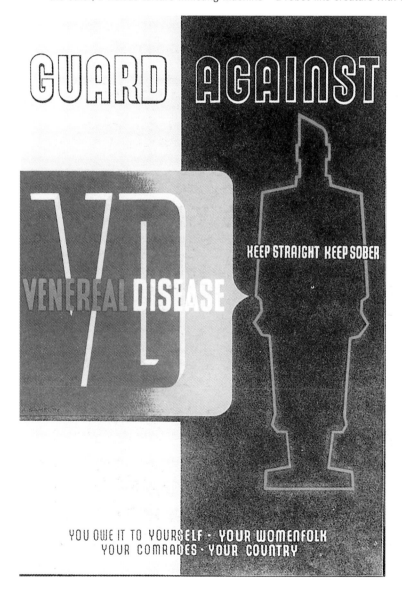

and many hands, holding implements such as a saw, hammer and hypodermic syringe, together with a devil's fork. The headline reads, 'He knew all the answers(?)'. There is the familiar strapline, 'Leave 'em alone', and the remainder of the copy quotes cliches. The first a *double entendre*, all are well known to the man in the poster and the men at whom the poster is targeted: 'You're not a man 'til you've had it', '3 day painless cure' and 'No worse than a cold'.

The brash atmosphere of American venereal disease propaganda oscillates between pervasive degradation of women and derision of those men who became infected. This was not peculiar to the American military in Britain, as evidenced by US Army attitudes to venereal disease in Italy towards the end of the war.[15]

27

Clean living is the real safeguard

The amateur, flippant and flagrantly sexist nature of the American servicemen's approach to venereal disease propaganda is starkly contrasted by the covert sexism and darkly moralistic and threatening atmosphere common to all aspects of the British Government's public information campaign, 'Let Knowledge Grow'. This atmosphere is achieved by professional designers' shadowy photographic imagery and condemnatory copy. The campaign's designers included Reginald Mount, employed by the Ministry of Information, and F.H.K. Henrion, commissioned on a freelance basis. Henrion confirmed that the campaign lacked direction. Although he and Mount knew each other quite well, there was no formal

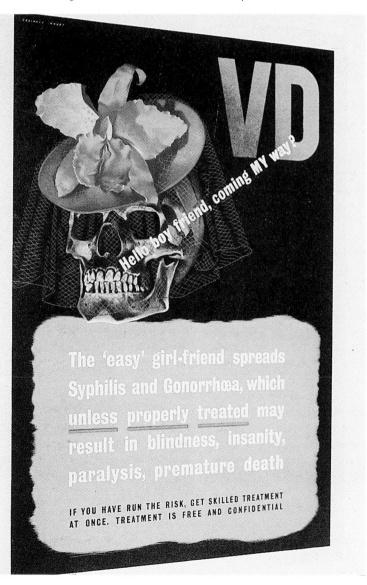

working relationship between the two designers, despite the fact that they were both engaged on the same project. According to Henrion, briefings were of the briefest kind and the results were limited: 'The posters did no more than make people aware; they didn't *explain* anything'.[16]

Some of the 'Let Knowledge Grow' material is very obviously sexist in that it shows women as the root cause of venereal disease and its distribution. A well-known poster by Mount depicts the head of a skeleton wearing an ostentatious hat with orchid and veil, together with the copyline, 'Hello boy friend, coming MY way?' This sexism, however, is not only far less overt than its American counter-part but, also, much of the material produced in the initial stages of the British campaign is almost devoid of the degree of sexism one may have anticipated. It is likely that a content analysis of the total campaign would reveal that the representation of women and men in this propaganda has, at least superficially, an unexpected balance and equality.

Some series of posters in the 'Let Knowledge Grow' campaign treat the subject of venereal disease in a gender-neutral way. The posters often include a child, together with either explicit or implicit representation of parental roles and responsibilities in connection with the disease. Parents are referred to in copy in the plural form and are visually depicted as a couple, insinuating joint and equal responsibility. Family values, clean living, fitness for parenthood and responsibility for tomorrow's citizen are strongly upheld in these posters. It is striking that responsibility is always laid equally at the door of both women and men. In gender terms, it is interesting to note that venereal disease is portrayed as adversely affecting men's *health* and women's *happiness*. Also, where a single child is referred to or depicted visually, it is always male – as in the 'Tomorrow's Citizen' poster, where an image of a lone small boy casts the shadow of a grown man. The copy reads, 'He must not be handicapped by Venereal Disease passed on by Parents. Make sure you're fit to be the Parents of tomorrow's citizens'. Another poster in the same series treats men as the cause and carriers of venereal disease and women and children as its victims. This poster pulls no punches in its message to men. Beneath a reversed-out silhouette of a bride, complete with long, flowing veil and confetti, and a large shadow image of two hands about to grasp the silhouette, the headline, 'here comes the bride', is supported by the following copy: 'A man suffering from Venereal Disease who infects his wife commits a violent crime against her and children yet unborn'.

Evidence suggests that the 'Let Knowledge Grow' campaign, together with the atmosphere surrounding the venereal disease issue as a whole in wartime Britain, was largely built upon *fear* – fear of the personal dangers of syphilis and gonorrhoea and of their ramifications for the family and, also, fear of the threat which these diseases posed to wider society and to the war effort. Much of this fear was internalized individually as a threat and was accompanied by guilt and moral panic. An ATS recruit recollects that

girls in the army became obsessed with the whole VD thing during the war, as it was drummed into you so much. Most of us had never heard of VD or knew what it was, but like many others I developed a discharge out of pure psychosomatic terror.[17]

A series of press advertisements, issued under the 'Let Knowledge Grow' umbrella in 1943 and each headed, 'From a Doctor's Diary', contains lengthy, anecdotal chat from 'the doctor'. With introductory copy such as, 'There are some things you just can't tell your wife, doctor',[18] these advertisements almost always make reference to 'loose living' or 'loose behaviour'. In the absence of practical information, frequent mention of the 'terrible consequences' or 'causes and terrible effects' of neglected venereal disease did more to frighten than inform.

Despite its name, the British 'Let Knowledge Grow' campaign, prompted by a near-epidemic of venereal disease and pressure from the American military, did little to help the growth of public knowledge. Described by the authorities at the

time of its launch in 1942 as 'the most intensive effort in the field of health education yet undertaken in this country',[19] the campaign barely mentioned the symptoms of venereal disease. When it did, references were invariably obscure. Despite its wartime 'intensive effort', at the end of the decade the Ministry of Health recognized that venereal disease was still a huge problem. In 1949, Abram Games was commissioned once again to design posters on the subject. Games recalls that the emphasis had changed:

By then, horror was disliked and Reggie Mount's posters had touched the limits of that approach. The accent was now on treatment and cure: warnings were considered inadequate, and people were still very much in need of positive information.[20]

People in wartime Britain were confused, frightened and angry: they wanted straightforward, factual information which, they believed, the Government should provide. Instead, government-imposed and euphemistic 'clean living', arguably unrealistic and impossible in time of war, was upheld as the only 'real safeguard'.[21] People resented the Government's promotion of a darkly moralistic campaign – a campaign outwardly concerned with sexually transmitted disease but implicitly concerned with sexual behaviour, and one which failed to provide any concrete information as to how to look for and recognize the symptoms of dreaded venereal disease.

Graphic Rebellion

Generation Terrorists: **Fanzines and Communication**

Teal Triggs

'...*people are building networks independent of big business, big governments, and big media. The zine world is in fact a network of networks.*'[1]

'*Send £1 plus the usual SASE...*'[2]

In July 1993, a new monthly magazine, *The Zine*, was introduced in Britain to provide a mainstream clearing house for information on DJs, club venues, new bands and album and concert reviews as well as other items of interest to the youth-orientated audience. *The Zine* has a cover price of £1.65 and is distributed widely, with issues readily available at newsagents and record stores on the British high streets. *The Zine* has adopted a standard 'magazine' format. It is printed on a slick A4 coated stock and stapled with conventional editorial sections, headlines and commercial advertising. It is a magazine, even by its own admission. *The Zine*'s cartoonist describes it as a 'Great Magazine Ya Gotcha Self Here!'. Despite its obvious affinity with standard magazine formats, *The Zine* draws heavily upon the written and visual language prevalent in 'fan' magazines or 'fanzines'. Its title is an abbreviation of 'fanzine', so acknowledging and reinforcing its debt to graphic 'fan' ephemera. Interestingly, by its appropriation of the visual and textual elements of fanzines within a conventional format, *The Zine* has unwittingly, or wittingly as the case may be, legitimized the fanzine form of subcultural graphic ephemera.

'Off the Page and into Print'[3]

The term 'fanzine' was first coined in the United States in 1949 to describe a mimeographed publication devoted primarily to science fiction and superhero comic enthusiasts. Fanzines have since come to embrace any subject faithful to the specific interests of 'fans'. They can focus either on 'personalities' (e.g. *I Hate Brenda*, spotlighting the character from the television series, *Beverly Hills 90210*), the music scene (e.g. *Ludicrous Line* for the band I, Ludicrous), sport (e.g. *Out of the Blue* for Colchester United F.C. fans), or issue-based topics (e.g. *Green Anarchist*, commenting on ecological ways to 'save the planet'). Cari Goldberg Janice describes what is now recognized formally as a fanzine:

Basically, a zine is anything that is published on a non-commercial basis. It can be called underground, or alternative, or independent. It has no limitation and is accomplished purely through individual blood, sweat and tears. Anyone can publish a zine – that's the main attraction.[4]

Fanzines operate within the realm of 'do it yourself' or amateur production.[5] Profit is rarely the motive for creating a fanzine, rather, its producers have a passion for their chosen subject, and this passion is primarily the fanzine's *raison d'être*.

As 'fandom' grew in popularity, communication between fans became inevitable as a means of creating cultural solidarity and a sense of community. Fanzines provided a focal point and unifying vehicle for establishing and reinforcing shared values, philosophy and opinions. Fanzines were easily and economically produced as photocopied, stapled A4 sheets. They were distributed primarily by post, and became a fundamental vehicle adopted by a number of independent publishers for communicating with like-minded individuals. Readers' letters to

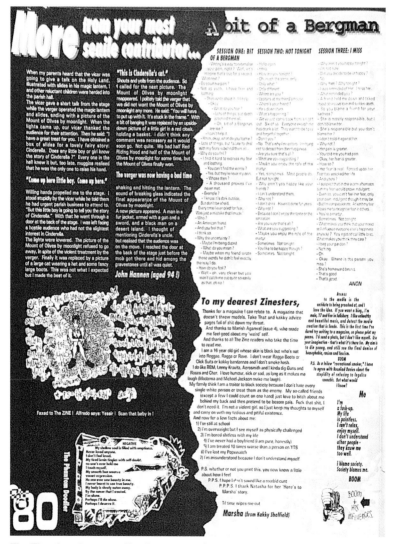

The Zine, interior page, Number 5, 1993/4

'Discussion' columns in early science fiction publications, such as Hugo Gernsback's *Amazing Stories* (c. 1926), as well as *Astounding* and *Wonder Stories*, provided the original impetus for these interactive forums for communication. One of the earliest printed fan communications in Britain was Maurice Hanson and Dennis Jacques' *Novae Terrae* (1936). This was soon followed by J. Michael Rosenblum's *The Futurian* (1938–40) produced in Leeds. It included 'fiction, poems and articles by leading sf [science fiction] fans of the day.'[6] Even today, the editor of *Peter Weller is Back* (1991), a revived fanzine that accompanied the relaunch of the singer's career, makes a plea for contributions and a continuous dialogue amongst fans: 'To keep *WIB* going I need the help of the readers through articles or interesting info'.[7]

One reason for the characteristic self-imposed anonymity of the reader/contributor is examined by the editor of *UK Resist* (1990):

The extended letter writing that comes from fanzine culture can fulfil a kind of fantasy role. Once immersed in it you can spend you[r] evenings 'talking' to your friends in other parts without the problems and inhibitions of real social contact. You can imagine your correspondents' appearance and character and feel like you really know them, without ever meeting.[8]

It is just such an informal and conversational approach that *The Zine*'s editorial policy seeks to emulate. In issue one of *The Zine*, the editor declares:

Express Yourself! The ZINE is created by its readers. It's for YOUR personal thoughts, photographs, artworks, cartoons, opinions, designs, stories, poetry, free ads, your anything! If you're not in…You're not in.[9]

Contributions including articles, book and record reviews and social commentary, as well as illustrations and comic strips, are submitted for publication by amateur writers and artists amongst its readership. Other readers are invited to comment through correspondence thus establishing a communication network between like-minded individuals. As a result, *The Zine* and its fanzine predecessors provide important unedited documents of subcultural activity specific to particular periods of time.

To further refine our understanding of the content and place of fanzines in contemporary culture, it is important to distinguish between the evolution of 'counter-cultures' and 'subcultures'.[10] Counter-cultures are essentially middle-class political alternatives to mainstream culture. They are typically issue-based such as gay liberation, women's rights, etc. Counter-cultures drive the alternative and radical presses. In contrast, subcultures are independent groupings exhibiting '…a distinctive enough shape and structure to make them identifiably different from their 'parent' culture.' Examples include the Mods, Rockers, Teds and Punks, all of which operated as distinctive groupings and all of which emerged from the working class.

The avant-garde raises special difficulties. In certain respects the avant-garde was never assimilated into mainstream activity. Instead it developed, as Raymond Williams further suggests,

...into alternative, more radically innovative groupings, seeking to provide their own facilities of production, distribution and publicity; and finally into oppositional formations, determined not only to promote their own work but to attack its enemies in the cultural establishments and, beyond these, the whole social order in their power.[11]

The avant-garde is subcultural and it is interesting that the form, content and graphic sensibilities of fanzines are derived from early twentieth-century avant-garde publications. The Situationists and Punk, much like members of Fluxus or the Dada Movement before them, sought to break down the artificial division of art and life, and thereby the division of low and high culture. They did so by questioning conventional ideas and practices in a variety of media including poetry, performance, music, painting and film, as well as typography and graphics. Due consideration must be given to those groups whose work offered both newness and confrontation, so establishing precedents for the production of contemporary British fanzines. Through the printed publications of the avant-garde, a recognizable visual language matured, reflecting the underlying constructs of each group. Man Ray's *Dadazine, The Ridgefield Gazook* (1915), and Ken Friedman's Fluxus-inspired *NYCS Weekly Breeder* (c. 1960) are examples that define the language (both visually and in writing) that was to come.

As we have seen, fanzines developed as amateur publishing networks for information exchange, for the development of implicit political manifestos and as opportunities for sharing critical responses to orthodox concepts of society and culture. Graphically, British fanzines received decisive impetus from the counter-cultural alternative and underground publications of the 1960s, but they crystallized with the subcultural Punk movement of the late 1970s.[12] Underground publications such as the *International Times* (*IT*, 1966) and *Oz* (1967) presented a literary, journalistic and visual document of the counter-cultural avant-garde, reflecting the inherent and often explicit political nature of their message. David Widgery, a frequent contributor to *Oz* , wrote in 1972 that '*Oz* dazzled with its eclecticism [and] *IT* became political in a most formal and unhelpful way...[13]

By contrast, Punkzines of the 1970s were usually devoted entirely to music and included record reviews, band profiles and interviews. But by the 1980s 'an awakening of political consciousness' had occurred in response to the world outside Punk.[14] At the same time though, market competition for an 'institutionalized' youth culture had grown, fostered in magazines such as *Time Out, i-D* and *The Face*. Stewart Home suggests that whereas the underground press of the 1960s had little or no competition for the youth market, the next decade proved more difficult, with commercial publications taking '...away a general youth audience for [Punk] 'zines such as *Sniffin' Glue* and *Ripped &Torn.*'[15] Despite these forces and a growing political consciousness, fanzine editors responded by providing their readers with further specialized music coverage, mirroring more closely the tastes of the 'small coteries of cultists.'[16] This in itself distinguishes fanzines from the youth culture publications of the last decade and gives force to Simon Frith's assertion that, 'The essence of fan mags is that they respond to tastes'.[17]

However, running in tandem to this growth in magazine publishing in Britain is the increased publication of and interest amongst readers for 'specialist' fanzines as a form of insurrection. Many fans are increasingly rebelling against magazines which impose particular sets of values, ideas and tastes on to their readership. Magazine zines, such as Michael Jackson's *Off The Wall* (c. late 1980s) and the Beastie Boys' *Grand Royal* (1993), represent 'official' mouthpieces of the singers' organizations and are used primarily as promotional vehicles. As a result,

37

Peter Weller is Back, cover, Number 1, 1991

they are less interactive than fanzines, opting instead to foster fan loyalty through carefully directed messages. The 1993/4 Winter edition of *Off The Wall*, for example, centres on providing evidence of Jackson's innocence in the face of allegations of sexual misconduct in recent press reports. Jackson fans are asked, amongst other activities, to '...write to the major newspapers and television networks demanding fairness in their reporting.... send a single white rose to Neverland, symbolising belief in his innocence.'[18]

Rebellion as graphic style

Fanzines represent and communicate the specific interests of both the fanzine

PAUL BEVOIR

THE BOSS

YEH YEH

THE SCENE

...clubs, gigs, news,

...and more !

Number 8   40p
November 85

GoGo, cover, Number 8, November 1985

producer and their audience through an assemblage of images, typeforms and commentary. In this way, they have developed their own language through specific coded terminology and usage as well as with visual imagery appropriated from popular media sources. The lexicon of type and imagery – cut-up ransom note lettering, graffiti handwriting and typewritten texts juxtaposed with newspaper photographs and childlike drawings – provides an essential common language for the 'community of consumers'. The idea of exclusivity is embodied in this development of a new language whose codes are only accessible to those who know and understand the language. Additionally, the fanzines often publish ideas and images without fear of censorship by a non-comprehending *status quo*.

As mouthpieces for rebellion, fanzines offer alternative critical spaces not accountable to the rules and conventions of mainstream publishing. In many cases, the actual design of the fanzine attempts to demonstrate the idea of rebellion by breaking conventional rules of typographic and visual communication. Based on the idea that 'anyone can do it', fanzines adopt printing techniques that are readily at hand and immediate to production. For example, early science fiction fanzines were either handwritten or involved using carbon paper to make multiple copies. As mechanical production technology developed, fanzine producers began to print copies using mimeograph, hectography and 'Ditto' machines and, more recently, photocopiers. The 'technofolksgraphik' of photocopied letterforms are authorized by the producers as recognized symbols of their own 'political' views and authority.

If anything, *The Zine* demonstrates how visual and verbal codes of rebellion formulated amongst street level communication networks, can be identified, appropriated, stylized and absorbed into mainstream culture. Ironically, these codes were often originally taken from mainstream media sources and subverted. The shock value embodied by the use of, for example, bad language, incorrect grammar, graffiti and ransom note texts, has become passive in its reading. What was originally proposed by fanzine editors to alienate those outside their intended audiences (as well as becoming an integral part of the image making process of rebellion), is now generally accepted and understood by the general public.

Today a plethora of new British fanzines have emerged alongside established titles such as *Boy's Own* (c. 1986) and *Raising Hell* (c. early 1980s). In addition to listings in *The Zine* (1993) and *Fact Sheet Five* (USA, c. 1982), monthly columns in *The Face* and *i-D* provide regular reviews of a variety of current fanzine titles. In the area of football alone, close to 400 fanzines are being produced which concentrate mainly on providing information on personalities and games for local football clubs. *When Saturday Comes* (c. 1986) is perhaps the most interesting phenomenon in the football zine category. Starting as a 12 page, A4, photocopied and stapled production which was distributed to about 100 fans, *WSC* circulation grew within a two year period to over 42,000. Although there has been an increase in the number of readers and pages and computer technology is now utilized, *WSC* has maintained its fanzine quality both visually and textually.

H.A.G.L. 19, interior page, Number 19, c. early 1990s

This has been generally true of fanzines that have used desktop publishing software. Texts still possess their cut and paste qualities. Computer typefaces have become simply an additional textural layer and have not been used to emulate standard mainstream typesetting.

Generally, fanzines have not been absorbed into the publishing mainstream. Their commitment to rebellion expressed as graphic style endures, though in a generally recognizable stylistic form as its elements are appropriated and recycled by the commercial market.

I don't know how to finish so i'm going to quote some words: 'Only we are the face of our time. The horn of time trumpets through us in the art of the word…The past is crowded…throw Pushkin, Dostoyevsjy, Tolstoy et al overboard from the ship of modernity.' (From 'A SLAP IN THE FACE OF PUBLIC TASTE' 1913). This is our generation. Do whatever feels right. Do it today.[19]

An extended version of this essay is published in part 3 of a special project of *Visible Language* 1995, 'New Perspectives: Critical Histories of Graphic Design'.

American Graphic Design for Social Change

Victor Margolin

Since the founding of the American colonies, visual images have played a role in the nation's political process, particularly by their representation of impulses for change. Whether these impulses have come from established groups or from radicals, their visual articulation has relied on changing codes, conventions and rhetorical forms for their political effectiveness.

Benjamin Franklin's political cartoon 'Join or Die', supposedly the first in America, was published in his newspaper, *The Pennsylvania Gazette*, in 1754. To convey the need for unity among the colonists in resisting the British, Franklin employed a metaphor, which was common for cartoonists at the time. The disunited colonies were depicted as a fragmented snake which needed to be joined together for its survival. By reducing an involved political situation to a single image, Franklin made an emphatic point to his readers.

Similar metaphors and documentation techniques were continued by artists who produced political prints in the nineteenth century. Many preferred lithography as a medium because it allowed a looser drawing style and eventually images in colour. With the introduction of mass circulation illustrated magazines after the middle of the nineteenth century, political images printed from engraved wood blocks helped boost sales by illustrating journalistic exposes of corruption. *Harper's Weekly* engaged cartoonist Thomas Nast, best known for his attack on New York City's crooked government headed by Boss Tweed in the 1860s and 1870s. Nast was instrumental in stereotyping rapacious city politicians as corpulent men who personified power by their sheer mass. He also developed pictorial devices to portray their greed, such as replacing a politician's head with a money bag. Similar graphic devices were used by other cartoonists. However, such stereotypes became worn out conventions through overexposure and eventually turned into political cliches as they were used repeatedly well into the 1930s.

Towards the end of the nineteenth century, various leftist movements – anarchist, socialist, and Marxist – began to spawn their own publications with such polemical titles as *Liberty*, *Alarm*, *New Nation* and *Social Crusader*. But none of them fully exploited the editorial power of visual images. An exception was *The Masses*, a monthly magazine which began publication in 1911 and continued until 1917. Distinct in its inclusion of politics within a larger cultural framework, its loose editorial policy provided some relief for writers and artists who were otherwise overly constrained by the radical journals of the time. Cover artists like John Sloan, a member of the group of American realist painters known as the

Ashcan School, depicted political events, while others simply conveyed images that pleased them.

In 1924, the American Communist Party started *The Daily Worker* which continued the pre-war stereotypes of fat capitalists, corrupt politicians, and war-mongering officers. The editors subordinated the artists to political directives and prevented the use of any visual material not intended to make a political point. When *The New Masses* was founded in 1926, it was intended to revive the cultural liveliness of its predecessor but ended up reflecting the hardline policies of the Communist Party. After the Comintern directed Communist parties in Europe and America to set up a Popular Front, the magazine's cartoonists dropped their stereotypes of exploited workers and businessmen with big cigars and began attacking fascists and racists. The magazine's leading cartoonist was William Gropper, whose scathing caricatures of political leaders recall the work of Daumier almost a century before.

The severe economic suffering caused by the Great Depression moved many artists, particularly those of the Left, to draw on that experience for their art. In depicting the overexploited and unemployed, artists often fell back on visual conventions such as the stooped shoulders of cotton pickers, or the ironic juxta-position of a breadline and an optimistic billboard that Margaret Bourke-White captured in a well-known photograph. While these conventions were not self-conscious stereotypes as were the figures in the *Daily Worker*'s cartoons, they were inflated into clichés from over-use.

Clenched fists and other dramatic polemical devices used by the Left were easily adapted for Second World War propaganda. In the immediate post-war years, Ben Shahn and other artists who had drawn war posters continued to use a vocabulary of political images that had been refined in the 1930s and in wartime. During the 1950s, when many on the Left were more cautious in their statements because of Senator McCarthy's Communist witchhunt, aggressive new approaches to advertising and magazine design were being developed in New York.

In the 1960s these developments were to result in a much more conceptual and less stereotypical way of making political statements which was a major break with the past. Such an approach also corresponded to a more independent politi-cal attitude particularly after the widespread disillusionment with the Soviet Union following the Stalinist purges of the 1930s.

The political and social changes of the 1960s were chronicled by George Lois on more than 90 covers which he art-directed for *Esquire*. Unlike Thomas Nast, William Gropper or Ben Shahn, Lois did not continue the conventional visual rhetoric of social change which, in the final analysis, was an artist's rhetoric that derived much of its power from drawing technique. Out were the raised fists, fat politicians, and downtrodden masses and in were shocking, irrev-erent and sometimes offensive conceptual images such as a hand wiping a tear from Kennedy's eye to illustrate Tom Wicker's attempt to write an objective mem-oir about the late President only seven months after his death. Likewise, an *Esquire* article on the masculinization of women was illustrated by a cover photograph of a beautiful woman shaving, an impossible image, but one that drove home a point like a sledgehammer.

Visually strong as Lois's covers were, *Esquire* was still a mainstream magazine which did not break the kind of stories that *Ramparts* did. It was founded in 1962 and its editor, Warren Hinkle, developed a style which he called 'radical slick'. Dugald Sturmer was the *Ramparts*' Art Director whose covers were as shocking as Lois's and gained additional power from the controversy of the investigative reportage and political exposes they illustrated. On one cover, for example, Sturmer ran a photograph of the *Ramparts*' editors holding up burning draft cards.

Strong graphic images could also be found in magazines that did not purport to represent the Left as *Ramparts* did. A good example is *Avant-Garde*, published and edited by maverick Ralph Ginzburg with Herb Lubalin as Art Director. *Avant-Garde*'s unholy combination of social concern and erotica made Ginzburg's eclectic agenda difficult to grasp. However, Lubalin contributed a new awareness of how typography could enhance a political statement. More general graphics by other well-recognized designers like Seymour Chwast and Milton Glaser added to a climate of change without directly referring to a specific situation or policy.

The popularity of posters by Chwast, Glaser and other designers testified to the growing power of images in American society. Such posters, by untrained as well as trained designers, proliferated in the 1960s as a protest against the Vietnam War and a response to a number of other causes. While some of these posters were intended for outdoor display, particularly on college campuses, many were commercially produced and were hung in private dwellings.

The images of fat capitalists, filibustering Congressmen, and warmongering generals, which had been the standard fare of leftist visual rhetoric in the 1920s and 1930s, no longer held the same power for a younger generation whose politics were shaped more by an intuitive sense of justice than by overarching ideological constructs. They preferred to subvert what they perceived to be symbols of domination such as the American flag. Graphics workshops were set up at universities and in communities to get posters out quickly, primarily by the inexpensive silkscreen method. Sometimes posters were even printed on cheap computer paper.

In the early 1960s, the foremost domestic issue was the struggle of black Americans for equal rights. But the period also saw a rise of other minority voices and this signalled a new plurality of special groups – blacks, women, hispanics, gays, Native Americans, and ecologists among them – that claimed their own political agendas. This growing concert of voices meant that political issues could no longer be represented in broad ideological terms and suggested that appropriate graphic statements would have to be found for each audience that was involved in a particular cause. In the 1960s, American graphic design was a predominantly white male enterprise and the new diversity of causes and groups posed a distinct challenge to the profession.

Humour continued to be an effective persuasive device for the Left in the 1960s because its aim was to subvert the policies and rhetoric of the

Establishment which the Right could only reproduce as given. One poster parodied a movie placard by describing the Vietnam War as an entertainment spectacle with Lyndon Johnson as its producer. Another ironically juxtaposed the name Johnson's Baby Powder, printed as it appeared on the company's packaging, with a photograph of a burned Vietnamese child. An additional example of subversion was the 1968 poster of a pregnant black woman wearing a button with Richard Nixon's presidential campaign slogan 'Nixon's the One'.

The rise of the women's movement during the late 1960s and the 1970s generated a new visual rhetoric that was initially based on militant symbols appropriated from other struggles but eventually moved towards the expression of a more subtle sensibility. *Ms.* magazine, originally co-founded and art-directed by the late Bea Feitler, was an important vehicle in the early 1970s for defining this sensibility. Feitler's covers were visually strong and synthesized a conceptual and decorative approach that incorporated popular culture, display typography, tropical colour, and many other influences.

Ms. gathered much of its support from women who were already in the mainstream, although it became a vehicle for bringing radical feminist ideology to a wider audience. But there were also small groups of feminist designers such as the Women's Graphic Collective in Chicago who created posters to promote solidarity among women and to express strident views of women's issues. Such groups portrayed the radical views within the women's movement without any need to tone them down for a mass audience.

Sheila de Bretteville put forth another approach to feminist design in 1982. As founder of the Women's Graphic Center at the Women's Building in Los Angeles, de Bretteville worked with many women who lacked professional training, helping them to express their own identities through graphic design. There is a connection between this process and the desire of Chicano poster artists who emerged in California during the late 1960s to reflect their own political struggles. Both groups were conerned with a sense of identity. Like the Chicano murals that artists began to paint around the same time, Chicano posters expressed a strong ethnic presence as well as the political aims of the Chicano and other Latino movements. They share some similarities with other posters and fine art of the period but are firmly rooted in the values of the bilingual bicultural Chicano community.

The resistance to mainstream media imagery since the 1960s has also been supplemented by other kinds of work that are based on the value of research and the cogent presentation of information. Good examples are the charts produced by Social Graphics, a research and design group in Baltimore which was founded in 1980. The aim of Social Graphics is to make information on demographic, economic and other social patterns accessible and comprehensible to people who are not statistically sophisticated, and the charts they produce enable the facts to speak for themselves.

However, many activists on the Left still hold the traditional belief that the word is more important for making political statements than the image. Until *The*

Masses appeared, most leftist editors paid little attention to art. And even after it folded, few subsequent radical publications gave any emphasis to their visual format. Among the exceptions is the independent socialist magazine *In These Times* which sustains visual interest in its layouts with typographic variety as well as the use of drawings and photographs.

Today, one of the most powerful impulses to create strong political graphics comes from AIDS activists, particularly the graphic artists associated with the national group ACT UP, which has used graphic images on posters, T-shirts, stickers and other media to spread a wider public awareness of AIDS related issues. Other political groups also make use of different graphic media to denounce injustices and promote their causes. There is currently a strong plurality of visual styles and rhetorical strategies which ensures that American protest graphics remain very much alive.

This article originally appeared in a considerably longer version in *Design Issues*, Vol. 5:1, Fall 1988. Reproduced courtesy of MIT Press.

Solidarity: **Subversive Codes in the Production of Political Change**

Diane J. Gromala

In 1980, in response to worsening economic conditions, corruption and political abuse, workers participating in the Lenin Shipyard strike in Gdansk, Poland, formed Solidarity, the first independent trade union in an Eastern Bloc country. A semi-legal organization from August of 1980 to December of 1981, Solidarity subsequently continued as an underground social and political movement. Its activities, characterized by a commitment to non-violence and subversive resistance to the harshly repressive Communist regime, eventually led in 1989 to the first democratic elections in a Communist country since 1946. The success of Solidarity is credited with setting the stage for other Eastern Bloc countries' claims for independence and the eventual dissolution of the USSR.

The production and dissemination of design played a primary role in the processes of this pluralistic mass movement of radical democratic change. From creation to distribution and response, the range of activities associated with design functioned in a complex variety of ways. First, it was one of the principal agencies of communication, in effect creating and reinforcing sites of contestation and, to a lesser degree, negotiation, among social, political and economic forces. Next, design facilitated the organization of the efforts of an estimated 9.5 million Solidarity members, that is, a majority of Poles, during the 1980s. The activities associated with design helped create a greater sense of community and nurtured revolutionary sentiment by building upon a strong Polish identity. Finally, design made available and distributed the documentation of civil rights abuses and the corruption of the Communist government, which was otherwise suppressed by official media sources.

In this context, design was a highly participatory and discursive activity, functioning both within existing structures as well as creating new ones, its strength and effectiveness deriving from its legacy of a subversive visual and verbal language. Solidarity's political influence during the 1980s produced rich and diverse examples of design as social, political and economic interaction: using traditional and subversive forms of production; engaging designers, writers, artists, governments and the populace at large.

Context

It is important to understand that the Solidarity movement occurred in a context radically different from that of so-called Western democracies. What was created in terms of graphic design in post-war Poland was to a large extent determined by government authorities, who both commissioned and controlled what was produced. This situation was restrictive in that it stifled initiative, freedom of expression and vision. It also reflected a crumbling economy, where items such as bread, soap and toilet paper were in chronically short supply. In such a context, the type of graphic design associated with a market-driven need to advertise and distinguish among product competition was unnecessary. In addition, protracted shortages of material and diminishing state support jeopardized the ability of designers and artists to work. However, the Communist government did regularly commission design for cultural events such as theatrical productions, cinematic runs, musical performances and museum exhibitions, which allowed Polish artists and designers a relatively fair amount of expressive freedom. In keeping with a long tradition of resistance to foreign domination, Polish artists and designers capitalized on this creative opportunity by further developing their matrix of powerful visual metaphors. Often characterized by satire, irony, paradox and dark humour, these metaphors allowed double or secret meanings to be encoded in what was deemed legally acceptable.[1] These poster commissions were in effect institutionalized support for professional designers. They further emphasized the international reputation of Polish poster design as a valued cultural tradition, and became a source of income for the state beyond the cultural events themselves.[2]

In addition to the differences in how graphic design was produced in non-market as opposed to market contexts, the understanding of the function of design in Poland also bears significant differences from the west. The perception of graphic design, particularly in the US, is frequently that it is merely an elitist tool of corporate interests. Issues often ascribed to Communist, totalitarian regimes assume different, less obvious forms in the west. Censorship in market economies, for example, is more often the result of social mores and market forces than of an authoritarian dictum. Moreover, the relative paucity of polemics and contextual analyses[3] of how design operates within market economies remains an area for exploration among designers themselves.

This frame colours common perceptions of graphic design, resulting in an inclination for designers in the west to marginalize the visual work produced by Solidarity as 'political art'. The assumption is that 'political art' bears little relevance to personal or direct experience. Also implicit is a paradox: although graphic design exists and operates within the social realm, many designers seem to accept only tacitly the notion that their work is important in intervening at many cultural levels, a 'failure determined by the intractability of the traditional idealist conception of art, which entirely divorces (art) from engagement in lived social life'.[4] With a few notable exceptions, such as work produced by ACT UP and related organizations confronting the AIDS crisis, work associated with the abortion debates and the Holocaust museum, overtly political design is rarely visible in the discursive practices of western designers. Further, the political aspects of design which are deeply embedded in western market economies merit exploration by designers. Work such as graffiti, 'vernacular' images, or visuals from rave and cyberpunk subcultures are rarely legitimized as graphic design. They are sometimes referred to, appropriated or commodified by professionally-trained designers, but only in stylistic terms, rarely in ideological ones.[5]

Perhaps the most important difference between design in the west and design produced by Solidarity in the 1980s is the question of what was at stake. The Poles are keenly aware of their legacy of keeping alive their language and cultural traditions in the face of centuries of devastating invasions and foreign rule, when at times Poland did not exist as a recognized country. Thus, during the 1980s, the production and use of graphic design and the symbolic codes of which it was comprised was a continuation of a long tradition, again in response to conditions that became essentially ones of self-determination and daily survival.

48

Creation

The Polish creation, production, distribution, interpretation, use of and response to what we can understand as graphic design raises questions about assumptions commonly held in the west. These include notions of singular heroic genius and originality; issues of appropriation and copyright; professional legitimacy and distinctions between artists and designers. These questions arise when we look at the processes of how and why these design works were created, and how they functioned within their specific context as viewed from a western perspective.

The creation of thousands of elements as diverse as posters, graffiti, books, arm bands, newspapers, pamphlets, badges, journals and photographs was undertaken by those trained as artists and designers, as well as by the populace at large, including factory workers, farmers, church officials and intellectuals. The urgent need to communicate during rapidly-changing circumstances and under conditions which discouraged this and outlawed public assembly superseded any demand for the creators to possess professional training or affiliation. The threat of imprisonment ensured anonymity.[6] In addition, the unity of intent and action of the three major groups which comprised Solidarity – the Church, workers and intellectuals – blurred boundaries between those who participated in art and those who were usually excluded. Underground art exhibitions and performances were held in factories, and were produced by artists and the factory workers themselves.[7] Exhibitions were also often held in churches, which were many times the only permissible venues for public assembly.

Stylistic appropriations became highly charged political issues. The pictorial style of posters created for Solidarity candidates in 1989, for instance, was quickly adopted by Communist candidates, who sought to confuse party affiliation. In response, Solidarity photographed their candidates shaking hands with Lech Walesa to ensure veracity of party affiliation, a claim to photographic truth that would be questionable in the west.

In the creation of visual works for Solidarity, the Polish populace drew on a common iconography: a set of images and symbols transmitted verbally and visually from one generation to the next which reinforced their cultural identity of resistance to foreign authority. This iconography derived from folklore, art, literature, ancient city and church symbols and aphorisms. Some of these visual metaphors were centuries old, while others developed during more recent times; some were based on visual references, and others on linguistic plays. Crows, for example, were used to depict the Communist secret police, as the acronym for their organization (Military Council of National Salvation) spelled WRONA, the Polish word for crow. A popular image during the 1980s, the crow was often seen or implied in an interplay with the Polish national emblem, the eagle.

The form of this iconography was generally mutable. Poses of figures in famous paintings for example, were repeatedly used by various Polish resistance movements. These were not necessarily exact replications of form, but were based on a communal memory of a pose or gesture as depicted in basic visual

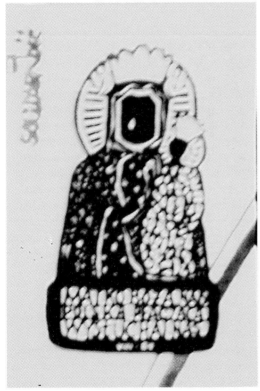

The Black Madonna. 'The Black Madonna' resides in a monastery in Czestochowa, considered the spiritual centre of Poland. The thirteenth-century icon is possibly Byzantine, and is attributed with mystical characteristics, often protective in nature. The Madonna is reputed to have issued blood when slashed by a Hussite soldier. In this depiction, she sheds a tear, a reference to a seventeenth-century Swedish invasion, when the icon was also reputed to have shed tears. Pope John Paul II made a pilgrimage to this monastery during a visit, enabling the global media access to the country during martial law. Lech Walesa often visited, seeking guidance and support through prayer, and frequently wore this commonly recognized symbol of mysticism and nationalism as a lapel badge.

narratives,[8] variable in form and shades of meaning. In one case, an image of a sailor at a ship's helm first appeared in poster form in 1940 to celebrate the working class at the helm of the state. Its incarnations during the 1980s included pictorial mutations of the sailor in various gestures of defiance; the meaning of 'worker at the helm' was retained, but the reference to the Communist party was not. The sailor was replaced in one version by a satirical rendering of a rather ragged Wojciech Jaruzelski, a 'Soviet general in Polish uniform'. The mutability of form was most visible in the ubiquitous use of the Solidarity logo itself, which visually recalls the Polish flag.[9] Its crudeness, which suggests both a sense of urgency and of being 'of the people', was also a necessary aspect of variability, as it was impossible to ensure consistent methods of reproduction. Moreover, the logo was adopted by other concerns of Solidarity; the specific letters exchanged for those of the farmer's union, cities, calls for boycotts and the like. The logo, which was reproduced with everything from ink and paint to chalk and neon, provided instant recognition and validation across many media, including television.

Production

The production of design work by Solidarity was difficult by any standards, as the totalitarian regime controlled mass media, not only through state ownership and censorship, but also through sanctions against access to or private ownership of technological means of reproduction, such as printing presses, photocopiers or fax machines. Materials needed for producing printed matter, such as ink, paper and photographic equipment, were often in short supply or controlled by the state. Needs were immediate, as work had to be produced quickly in order to respond to rapidly changing conditions. Thus the entire body of technological reproductive methods and materials needed to be accessed and used in all ways imaginable to achieve Solidarity's objectives.

In one case recounted by prominent design historian and former Solidarity activist Dr Szymon Bojko,[10] activists would hide disassembled parts of a printing press in their homes, as it was illegal to own an entire printing press. They would then meet and assemble the press to print books, pamphlets, journals, and other materials covertly and in a short period of frenzied activity, disassembling the press and again concealing the parts immediately afterwards. At several times during martial law, access to technology was so restricted that writers used valuable carbon paper over and over, painstakingly manually typing books on paper smuggled from East Germany or the west. The illicit books were distributed underground, hand to hand. Because various technologies were sporadically outlawed in Poland during the 1980s, work can usually be dated by determining which technological means of production was used.

Distribution

The distribution of Solidarity's communiques was often a combination of intervention in official distribution systems and the continual creation and recreation of underground systems. Subverting official venues, imprisoned activists embroidered information on to prison shirts, which were smuggled out by launderers. Postal

50

workers developed a system to identify and mark which mail had gone uncen-
sored within the official postal system, while a parallel underground network of
distribution also developed. Likewise, other Solidarity members marked circulating
money, and also created a system of unofficial currency. Solidarity activists also
openly challenged official systems. Censorship for example, was confronted by take-
overs of a television station and jammings of its transmissions. Walls in prominent
areas were often venues for graphic information withheld by the authorities: photographs documenting beatings of political prisoners, listings of those recently
arrested or missing, as well as pictorial graffiti, manifestos and mementos. One of
these walls in Warsaw was repainted by the Communist authorities every morning

**Poczta Podziemna (Underground Mail). This creation offers an oblique reference to a
seventeenth-century painting that porrays a peasant looking over his shoulder; a
reminder to be vigilant and careful of the ever-present watchfulness of the authorities.
Hunched in covert mid-delivery of underground mail, this more animated figure looks
over his shoulder to a Soviet spaceship – the watchfulness of the authorities now
extended to an omnipresent surveillance system.**

only to be covered again with Solidarity materials by noon. Information was pasted
and taped to windows, walls, pavements, cars and monuments, even on trains
destined for rural locations.

Solidarity's communiques were intended to facilitate communication among
the Polish people themselves, but also to garner world support through the media.
The 'first rebellion in history to be played out under the scrutiny of television cameras',[11] Solidarity consciously formed and organized its visibility for both functions.

During papal visits, crowds arranged flowers into the form of a cross on a monumental scale – a moving visual image of the peaceful resistance of the Poles, especially as the riot police dispersed the crowd in front of the world's media. In another case, the Solidarity logo was spray painted onto a pig which was released into a crowd, an effective way of gaining the attention of foreign correspondents.

The elaborate unofficial systems of distribution were rooted in networks that took form in response to the civil unrest in 1968 and 1970, and were established with the co-operation of intellectuals and the Church. Following the repression of a workers' strike in 1976, the intellectuals formed KOR (Workers' Defence Committee), the goal of which was to provide material and legal support to workers who were fired or had civil rights violated. Its ethos of 'scrupulous honesty, nonviolence and forbearance, plus a reluctance to sit in judgement, echoed the basic tenets of Christianity',[12] – in other words, KOR had a great deal of common ground with the Church. Its 'Flying University' organized lectures on forbidden and controversial subjects in private homes and was a source of banned and semi-legally published information.

Although once a country of diverse religious and ethnic groups, the Second World War left Poland 90 per cent Catholic and ethnically Polish. Historically, the Church was conflated with nationalistic sentiment and functioned as a safe haven in maintaining a distinct Polish cultural identity in the face of imposed 'official' histories and languages. Solidarity unified the complex web of subversive systems, responsive underground infrastructures and subeconomies developed by the Church, intellectual groups, and trade organizations. Because open confrontation with Communist rule would almost assuredly result in brutal military repression, Solidarity's intent was to undermine the authority of repressive rule through the daily practice of networks of resistance and refusal, living '"as if" Poland were already a free society'.[13] Such a philosophy, supported by a fluid infrastructure, worked to invite the participation of the majority of Poles in their struggle toward self-determination.

Consequences

Although it represented a dominant group in terms of population, in terms of power relations Solidarity functioned as a subculture within the strictures of the repressive Communist regime's state sponsorship. By methods of generally peaceful resistance, Poles went to the streets, at once to organize and support themselves, and also to put forward their cause in front of the eyes of global media. Utilizing elaborate subversive methods, which often assumed material forms that can be understood as graphic design, Solidarity succeeded in garnering world support at a crucial time, and achieved their aims of self-determination and open, democratic elections.

Yet, as events at the time of writing point toward the possible re-election of former Communist candidates, re-organized,[14] many questions remain. What form of democracy and economic system will be adopted in Poland? What happens to a culture whose identity is based on resistance when the object of resistance is

**W SAMO POŁUDNIE
4 CZERWCA 1989**

Election poster: High Noon, Tomasz Sarnecki, 1989. The most popular poster of the elections of 1989 references the American film of 1952, High Noon. In the film, Gary Cooper is the sheriff who courageously, if reluctantly, stands against insurmountable odds in the form of armed and vengeful outlaws. In this poster, Cooper stands ready to confront the Communist outlaws, armed not with a gun but a ballot for Solidarity. This depiction has Solidarity aligned with the specifically American icon and mythology of the 'good guy' cowboy: a brave, rugged individualist standing alone, fearless. At the end of the movie, a victorious Cooper throws his badge in the dirt in disgust and rides off with his bride, a non-violent Quaker, to run a store – or a market economy. The cowboy was a prevalent theme: Walesa referred to himself as a sheriff, while graffiti often depicted the Communist opposition as 'Indians' with headbands and feathers. However, adopting the romantic notions of Hollywood wholesale is problematic, as the myth also carries dark connotations such as racism, patriarchal colonialism, violence and environmental exploitation.

removed? Mass and electronic media are often blamed, in part, for the inability of totalitarian regimes to maintain power. If so, what effect will participation in global market economies have on Poland's ability to maintain its cultural identity? Will the Poles, already attuned to recognizing multiple and hidden meanings, as well as having a propensity to understand paradox, use these attributes to resist the homogenizing effects of an increasingly global economy and attendant electronic technologies?

The changing economic context in the current move toward a market economy may significantly alter the practice of Polish design. The history and international reputation of the distinctive Polish poster tradition, for example, is honoured as a national treasure and connected to a lived reality. That 'lived reality' traditionally finds a venue for expression in Polish design, no matter what significant changes in conditions may occur. However, Polish designers themselves express concern that severe economic conditions will jeopardize the tradition, as government sponsorship of poster design for cultural events no longer exists. Because of cost considerations, Polish posters have been replaced with the material that generally accompanies imported cultural events.[15]

While these questions are played out, it is useful to see that the context and processes of the design produced by Solidarity cannot be easily understood or valued simply by formal analysis. Designers are cultural producers, affecting and in turn, being affected by culture. If we can begin to understand the political aspects embedded in our western market economies as part of everyday life, in the sense that design affects us, we will be better able to become responsible participants in the process.

Organizing a Counter-culture with Graffiti: **The Tsoi Wall and its Antecedents**

John Bushnell

In late August 1990, graffiti celebrating and mourning Viktor Tsoi appeared on the wall of a short byway leading off the Arbat pedestrian mall in central Moscow. Tsoi, one of the most popular Soviet rock stars, had died in a car crash outside Riga on 15 August. The Arbat was a gathering spot for hippies, punks and other members of the Soviet counter-culture, who were already making their mark on the walls of the Arbat and its branching courtyards and alleys. Thus it was a large but not startling gesture when they appropriated a 100 foot stretch of wall, covered it with graffiti memorializing Tsoi, christened the byway Viktor Tsoi Alley, and on 25 September – the fortieth day after Tsoi's death, when in Russian Orthodox tradition friends and relatives hold a memorial feast for the deceased – formally dedicated the wall.

The Viktor Tsoi wall (as it immediately became known) was both a culminating and a concluding statement by the Soviet counter-culture. Graffiti had been central to the organization of a counter-culture throughout the 1980s.[1] Because Russian rock fans and counter-culture groups had for some time been appropriating public spaces and devoting them to written and pictorial statements of their own cultural preferences, they knew that the proper way to mark Tsoi's passing was to cover a wall with graffiti honouring him. As they had already established themselves in the public arena, they could do so with impunity. In 1983 or 1985, Moscow's municipal authorities would have successfully resisted the effort to memorialize Tsoi on the Arbat; even in 1988 the police would have contested, albeit weakly, the counter-culture's efforts. But by 1990, the counter-culture through sheer persistence had won the right to hang out in the Arbat – and in many other places – and the creation of the Tsoi wall was accepted as a matter of course.

The direct ancestors of the Tsoi wall were stairwells covered with graffiti devoted to Mikhail Bulgakov and Boris Grebenshchikov. Bulgakov was a writer who had died in 1940, and had been largely forgotten until the publication of his masterpiece, *The Master and Margarita*, in 1965. That novel could not have been published in the 1930s when Bulgakov wrote it, and its publication even in the more liberal 1960s was surprising. The novel recounts three intersecting stories: the visit of Satan (Woland in the novel) and his troupe to Moscow, the story of the crucifixion as written by the Master and the persecution of the Master, whom Woland finally rescues from a lunatic asylum. The novel is thematically complex, but also enormously popular across the entire spectrum of the reading public.

The graffiti demonstrated that it was the novel's carnivalesque elements – the bedevilment of officials and the cultural establishment by Woland's assistants – that most strongly attracted the reading public, or at least that part of the public which contributed graffiti. Of the many sites in Moscow associated with the novel, the only one honoured with graffiti was a flat in which Bulgakov himself had once briefly lived and which, very lightly disguised, Woland took over during his Moscow sojourn. Graffiti first appeared in the stairwell in mid 1983, and within a year the walls leading up to the fifth floor flat were so thick with overlapping inscriptions that most individual contributions were no longer legible. Their message was clear none the less: the drawings were almost entirely of the tricksters

Tsoi wall, September 1990

who were the agents of devilment; the quotations from the novel (aside from exclamations of admiration for Bulgakov, quotations were the most numerous graffiti) were mostly the tricksters' best lines. Through the deployment of quotations, the graffiti writers endorsed the novel's challenge to Soviet cultural verities.

The graffiti in the Bulgakov stairwell constituted activity as well as text. The stairwell was, in its early years, contested space. Residents hated what was happening and repeatedly summoned the police, who proved no permanent deterrent to gatherings of graffiti writers. The housing administration repeatedly painted the stairway walls, but the writers treated this as an offering of so much fresh canvas, and recreated the collection every time – always with the carnivalesque themes at the centre, but with an accompaniment of other elements drawn from the evolving repertoire of counter-culture themes and symbols. As early as 1984, the fame of the stairwell had spread to cultural and counter-cultural circles in St Petersburg, then named Leningrad, and legends had grown up around it. Within a year or so, the Bulgakov stairwell was a counter-cultural pilgrimage site. In 1986 the authorities gave up their attempt to police the stairwell, and in 1988 agreed to turn the Bulgakov apartment into a museum.

Meanwhile, in St Petersburg in 1984 or 1985, graffiti began to accumulate in the stairwell leading to the apartment of Boris Grebenshchikov, at the time Russia's most renowned rock musician – St Bob, as some of the graffiti styled him. Grebenshchikov had long been active in the Russian rock music underground; Soviet authorities had not been able to suppress or domesticate rock music, and by harassing rock musicians and denying them access to legitimate venues they

Tsoi wall, September 1990

themselves had helped to turn rock music into a subversive art. But the graffiti in the Grebenshchikov stairwell was not just a tribute to an underground rock idol: it, like the Bulgakov graffiti, created a sacred space; a magnet for the counter-culture and other disaffected young people, a pilgrimage site for counter-cultural wanderers. The number of groups (identifiable by name and symbol) contributing to the collection was quite impressive, as was the number and distance of the cities from which fans had come to pay Grebenshchikov tribute. This stairwell, too, had been taken over by and made to represent cultural opposition.

Despite the enormous differences between a literary masterpiece and even very good rock music, the writers of the graffiti explicitly linked Grebenshchikov with Bulgakov, and both of them to the hippy-centred counter-culture. By 1988, there were tributes to Grebenshchikov and quotations from his lyrics in the Bulgakov stairwell in Moscow, even a graffito announcing that 'IF BULGAKOV

HADN'T BEEN KILLED BY STALIN, HE WOULD LISTEN ONLY TO AQUARIUM' (the name of Grebenshchikov's group). At other counter-culture sites, too, graffiti honoured both Bulgakov and Grebenshchikov, and placed both firmly within the small counter-culture pantheon.

The Bulgakov and Grebenshchikov stairwells – like the Tsoi wall later – were part of an emerging geography of cultural opposition, a network of sites taken over by the counter-culture. Graffiti invariably identified these sites and turned them into statements of principles and values. The network grew rapidly during the Gorbachev years, as public authority grew more tolerant – or decrepit. By 1988, the counter-culture geography included: an enormous rotunda four stories high in St Petersburg that hippies had turned into a hangout which boasted poems and philosophical statements; a series of interconnecting courtyards in central Moscow devoted entirely to Beatles' graffiti (the Beatles were greatly esteemed by Russian hippies and pacifists); and numerous other counter-culture hangouts with their own smaller but distinctive accumulations of graffiti. As of 1988, graffiti devoted to Viktor Tsoi and his group Kino were popping up here and there, but they sounded a very minor note in the babble of pacifist, punk, hippy and rock fan inscriptions.

Counter-culture groups employed graffiti to claim space and announce their rejection of Soviet society, but they were not the first to use graffiti for those purposes. That honour goes to the *fanaty*, youth gangs that appeared in Moscow in the late 1970s, who took local football teams as their totems and fought other gangs with different totems. They invented graffiti as a mode of public expression in the Soviet Union: their graffiti claimed territory, celebrated the gangs and their totemic teams and denigrated their rivals. The most significant feature of gang graffiti was the employment of English words and symbols originating in English, such as the V for victory hand signal, to exalt gangs and totems, and Russian only to denigrate their enemies. The graffiti grammar thus encoded a cultural judgement: English was the language of honour because the popular culture associated with it was infinitely more appealing and prestigious than the insipid official Soviet offerings. Quite unconsciously, the *fanaty* made public graffiti from the beginning a weapon not just of opposition, but of cultural subversion.

Other disaffected groups of young people – devotees of heavy metal music, of the Beatles and rock music in general, hippies, pacifists, punks – followed suit. They too employed graffiti to establish a public identity and, more explicitly than the *fanaty*, to proclaim their antipathy to official Soviet culture. They adopted much of the gangs' symbolic vocabulary, and in many of their graffiti they employed the same culturally-charged grammar. The result was that all of the disaffected youth groups, from the rough football gangs to the deliberately passive hippies, formed a linguistic community united by the employment of a graffiti argot that only they could understand. The counter-culture creation of graffiti-stairwells and graffiti-walls beginning in 1983 was innovative, but it drew on the weight of cultural opposition that public graffiti had carried from the beginning. Quite apart from their explicit message, any assemblage of graffiti proclaimed: heterodox, non-conformist, un-Soviet.

Tragic death lifted Viktor Tsoi into the cultural opposition's pantheon, and like Bulgakov and Grebenshchikov before him he was honoured with his own memorial wall. By 1990, it was possible to create the memorial with dispatch and in full public view. The Tsoi wall is of interest chiefly as artefact: a sacred site in a cultural system that had grown up in opposition to the dreary Soviet product, a space necessarily marked by devotional graffiti understood to represent specific values and attitudes.

The Tsoi wall graffiti themselves are quite banal, especially in comparison with the rich expression at earlier counter-culture sites. 'VITIA (Tsoi's nickname), WE'RE WITH YOU', or alternatively, 'VITIA, YOU'RE WITH US'; 'VIKTOR, WE LOVE YOU'; 'VITIA (such and such a city, many are mentioned) WILL REMEMBER YOU'; 'VITIA'S ALIVE, BUT HE'LL ALWAYS BE 28; WE WON'T FORGET YOU!!' – these and other such declarations, differing only in the size of the lettering, make up the bulk of the inscriptions. A few declarations and symbols associated with particular groups – 'PIPLY', that is the 'people', as many hippies refer to themselves; 'LIU-BERA', the working class toughs from the Moscow suburb of Liubertsy – maintain the tradition that all the disaffected youth groups come together at sacred sites. A graffito employing 'remember' in English harks back to the honorific linguistic stratum in graffiti argot. A few portraits of Tsoi and the inscription christening this Viktor Tsoi Alley, by now cliches at counter-culture sites – and that just about exhausts the inventory. The entire assemblage is derivative and mechanical. There is nothing in the graffiti that might explain, for instance, why Tsoi was popular, or what it was he was thought to have stood for.

Tsoi was in fact a major figure in late Soviet popular culture. Some of his songs became youth anthems, and he had an enormous following. But he could not occupy quite the same place in the oppositional culture that Bulgakov, or Grebenshchikov, or the Beatles, or even heavy metal music had occupied in the early 1980s, because by the time Tsoi became prominent, the cultural opposition had left the underground and almost entirely supplanted the Soviet creation that had once passed for popular culture. Tsoi released albums that sold millions of copies, went on tour (unsuccessfully) in Western Europe, and performed – even starred – in movies. Tsoi's history was not unique: in the late 1980s many formerly oppositional, underground rock bands enjoyed commercial success, and many charismatic rock stars debuted in films. All that was left of the once oppositional culture was an attitude and an aura that no longer represented the real cultural alignment.

Probably this is why the Tsoi wall was both a major achievement of the counter-culture and a clear sign that a once creative movement had gone stale. The wall demonstrated the triumph of the oppositional cultural practices, but there was no longer anything to oppose, no tension, no spur to creativity.

New Visions and Technology

Post-Photography: **The Highest Stage of Photography**

Kevin Robins

The death of photography is being widely reported. There is a gathering sense that we are now witnessing the birth of a new era, that of post-photography. This, of course, represents a response to the development of new digital electronic technologies for the registration, origination, manipulation and storage of images. Over the past decade or so, we have seen the increasing convergence of photo-graphic technologies with video and computer technologies, and this convergence seems set to bring about a new context in which still images will constitute just one small element in the encompassing domain of what has been termed hypermedia.[1]

What is happening – whatever it may amount to – is generally interpreted in terms of technological revolution, and of revolutionary implications for those who produce and consume photographic products. From such a perspective, old technologies, both chemical and optical, have come to seem restrictive and impoverished, whilst the new electronic technologies promise to inaugurate an era of almost unbounded freedom and flexibility in the creation of images. This tech-nological revolution is understood, furthermore, to be at the very heart of a broader cultural and intellectual revolution: no less than the historical transition from the condition of modernity to that of postmodernity. The postmodern order is felt to be one in which the primacy of the material world over that of the image is contested, in which the domain of the image has become autonomous, even in which the very existence of a 'real world' is called into question. Thus, the techno-logical developments of post-photography are drawn into a cultural mythology which imagines and projects the world as a 'post-real' technosphere – it is Jean Baudrillard's new world of simulation and simulacra, William Gibson's new dimen-sion of cyberspace.[2]

This notion of technocultural revolution has been widely accepted and celebrated by cultural critics and practitioners, and such ready acceptance has tended to inhibit critical engagement with post-photography. Indeed, it has encouraged a great faith in the new digital technologies, based on the expecta-tion that they can empower their users and consumers. A great deal of what passes for commentary or analysis amounts to little more than a simple and unthinking progressivism, unswerving in its belief that the future is always supe-rior to the past, and firm in its conviction that this superior future is a sponta-neous consequence of technological development. The fact that technological development is seen as some kind of transcendent and autonomous force –

rather than as what it really is, that is to say, embedded in a whole array of social institutions and organizations – also works to reduce what is in reality a highly complex and uneven process of change to an abstract and schematic teleology of 'progress'. The idea of a revolution in this context serves to intensify contrasts between past (bad) and future (good), and thereby to obscure the nature and significance of very real continuities.

What might constitute an alternative perspective on post-photography? How might we better assess its significance? In this brief discussion, I will address two issues: first, the cultural-aesthetic implications of digital technologies; and, then, the question of the social institutions in and through which these implications are being taken up and explored. In considering these issues, I shall tend to emphasize the continuities more than the discontinuities between photography and post-photography. I shall also argue that, whilst certain possibilities are, indeed, being opened up by post-photographic technologies, their realization is far from being a matter of course. Whatever happens, for good or for ill, can only be a consequence of deliberations, judgements and decisions that are made by all those involved in the development and applications of the new post-photographic technologies.

In terms of the cultural and aesthetic expectations that are being invested in digital technologies, what come across most forcefully in journalistic and academic commentaries are claims about the expanded 'creativity' they will permit. There is the sense that photography was constrained by its inherent automatism and realism, that is to say, by its essentially passive nature; that the imagination of photographers was restricted because they could aspire to be no more than the mere recorders of reality. In the future, it is felt, the enhanced ability to process and manipulate images will give the post-photagapher greater 'control', while the capacity to generate virtual images through computers, and thereby to make images independent of referents in 'the real world', will offer greater 'freedom' to the post-photographic imagination. What is 'superior' about the post-photographic future becomes clear, then, through contrast with what is seen as an inferior, and obsolete, photographic past.

But, of course, technological progressivism creates too simplistic a contrast between past and future. Let us be clear that photographers have always sought, in their different ways, to fracture and dislocate our vision of reality, often with the express aim of contributing to the political or cultural transformation of that reality. To this end, there was always significant resistance to automatism and realism, and, of course, the manipulation and processing of the images has always been central to photographic practice. Photomontage is one very obvious example. The Dada artist Hannah Höch, writing in the 1930s, traces photomontage back to the origins of the photographic medium:

The first instances of this form, i.e., the cutting and rejoining of photos or parts of photos, may be found sometimes in the boxes of our grandmothers, in the fading, curious pictures representing this or that great-uncle as a military uniform with a pasted-on head…Another picture might show us a ready-made landscape, perhaps a boat on a picturesque lake bathed in moonlight, with an entire family group pasted on that scene.[3]

In the 1920s and 1930s, photomontage was turned to more serious ends. Höch herself is extremely positive about the artistic potential of this technique, which she believes 'opened up a new and immensely fantastic field for a creative human being; a new, magical territory, for the discovery of which freedom is the first pre-requisite'. At the same time, when she argues that 'photomontage continues to be the best aid for photoreportage', Höch also emphasizes its great significance for

Hannah Höch: 'Das schöne Mädchen' (The Beautiful Girl) (1919–20)

political and public intervention in the world's events, the work of John Heartfield being perhaps most famous in this respect.[4]

The simple point that I want to emphasize is that photography has always had a complex and contradictory relationship to the reality that it has been committed to represent. In her book, *On Photography*, Susan Sontag has described this in terms of an ambivalence, which has been manifest in the co-existence of conflicting ideals: 'assault on reality and submission to reality'.[5] To assume that the photographic past was only about submission, and then perhaps to be seduced into believing that post-photography could be all about assault, is simply facile. Over the past 150 years, photography has been implicated and involved in the world in complex ways, and the implication of post-photography will, necessarily and ineluctably, be equally complex.

Digital technologies do not of themselves suddenly and fundamentally change the cultural or political agenda. The artist and photographer Calum Colvin demystifies things and puts them in their proper perspective: 'it's important to say that the computer has just made things easier. It has extended the facility of being able to do certain things. But look at what John Heartfield could do with his means'.[6] Of course post-photography opens up new technical possibilities, and we have every right to be as hopeful about these techniques as Hannah Höch was about those of photomontage, but we should not become infatuated with the tools at the expense of what must be done with them. They cannot guarantee 'creativity' or 'empowerment', even if there are those who continue to indulge in such Promethean expectations. The significance – I would even say the relevance – of digital technologies can only be in relation to the worth of the cultural and political projects through and for which they are mobilized. In developing these projects, we should recognize important continuities with the projects of Höch, Heartfield and a great many others, and not delude ourselves into believing the 1990s constitute a new beginning, year zero of virtual reality.

The question concerning new digital technologies has become caught up in a cultural agenda, at once romantic and utopian, about the exploration and conquest of cyberspace. This has given rise to debates about ontology and epistemology, about reality and hyperreality, about the shift from modernity to post-modernity, about whether human beings are mutating into cyborgs. Out of fictitious imaginings and philosophical abstraction have come blueprints for new worlds, new realities, new historical eras. Now I am not against philosophical speculation about the condition of postmodern existence, anymore than the next person. But I am not convinced that this takes us very far in understanding the significance of post-photographic technologies. Perhaps it seems rather too sober an objective, but I would argue that all this needs to be grounded in more mundane realities. What is needed is a more *sociological* account, one that takes account of the social and historical context in which both post-photography and post-photographic (or postmodern) discourses are being elaborated.

This brings me on to the second issue I want to take up in this discussion: the question of the institutions in and through which digital technologies are being developed and applied. For post-photography does not exist in the heavens as some kind of ideal Platonic form. Post-photographic practices are embedded in a whole array of organizations and businesses – press, media, advertising, design, leisure and entertainment, and so on – and are evolving according to the particular objectives and requirements of those various institutions. And when it comes to how the new technologies are imagined, let us remind ourselves that even postmodern imaginations are embedded in particular institutions – those of publishing, media, education – and reflect particular concerns of those particular institutions. In the process by which new technologies are being introduced into different organizations, it may be the case that certain practices are transformed,

Calum Colvin: 'ANGER' (1993), from 'The 7 Deadly Sins and the 4 Last Things'

but it does not follow at all that the established priorities or values of these organizations as a whole will be significantly changed in consequence.

The merit of an institutional perspective is to draw attention to the social and economic context that shapes, constrains and absorbs the innovation process. In many discussions of post-photographic developments, it is as if it were simply a matter of the individual interacting with a new tool that will enhance his or her individual creativity and control. The reality, however, is that individuals generally operate within collectivities, within divisions and hierarchies of labour, within organizations governed by logics (for example, efficiency, speed, cost-cutting) that may well be at odds with the values of individual expression or empowerment. The priority for an organization is to subordinate and direct the potential of new technologies according to its broader strategic needs.

Let us consider what this means in more concrete terms through two brief illustrations. In the case of design work, it is clear that digital technologies open up wholly new possibilities for the use of images and for their integration into other aspects of design. But on what basis these possibilities will be realized is quite another matter. In principle, the creativity of the individual could be enhanced. In practice, what is more likely is the enhancement of the overall creative output of a particular company at the expense of the individual creativity of many or most of its employees. The new technologies facilitate the fragmentation of tasks, the de-skilling of certain design workers at the same time as the re-skilling of others and the automation of many processes, as has been the case in computer-aided design. And if the enhancement of creativity is a prospect for certain designers, we should not assume, even for them, that this will automatically be the case. For, as David Bailey puts it bluntly, the new technology 'could breed mediocrity as it makes everyone slightly better than they are'.[7] Digital technologies will change design practices, they will improve technical quality, but in and of themselves, they do not and cannot guarantee greater creativity. That will depend on quite other conditions and circumstances.

The case of photojournalism, my second illustration, is also highly instructive.[8] Here, too, there is a significant issue to do with professional skills, demarcations and practices. What we see is a tendency for the autonomy and expertise of the photojournalist to be increasingly undermined as more and more aspects of the photographic process can be 'post-produced' in the computer. There is consequently a shift in the balance of power and responsibility from the photographer to the picture desk and the editorial room. In this professional domain, however, achievements in the digital manipulation of images are also raising a whole other set of issues. The achievement of post-photography has been to call into question the reliability and the veracity of the photographic record, and this has begun to open up profound dilemmas surrounding the ethical and moral basis of photojournalism as a profession. Of course, the authenticity of the image has always been an issue: as I have already suggested above, photography has never been, and could not be, simply a passive registration of events, even if it was often mistakenly thought to be so. None the less, provoked by the technological leap of post-photography, the problem of truth in representation is now posed in a new and more radical sense. The question photojournalism now faces is whether, on the basis of accepting and coming to terms with the instability of photographic meaning, it will be possible to elaborate a new or revised set of principles that will allow it to sustain critical and reflexive engagement with the world's events.

In conclusion, then, let us acknowledge that we are at a significant, perhaps critical, moment in the history of the photographic image. I very much agree with William Mitchell when he argues that the emergence of digital imaging now gives us the opportunity 'to expose the aporias in photography's construction of the visual world, to deconstruct the very ideas of photographic objectivity and closure, and to resist what has become an increasingly sclerotic pictorial tradition.'[9] I would strongly resist, however, the schematic logic that then goes on, all too easily, to construct a false polarization with the photographic past, now associated with disappointment and rejection, and the post-photographic future, evoking feelings of hope and expectation. It is as facile to dismiss old technologies and practices wholesale as it is crass to embrace new ones wholeheartedly. I have preferred in this discussion to stress the continuities between photography and post-photography. The emergence of digital imaging does not open up entirely new agendas, but rather, provides new basis for taking further the agendas that were originally opened up by the photographic image. In this sense, post-photography might be seen as the highest stage of photography.

Turning on to Television

Michèle-Anne Dauppe

Though barely acknowledged, except by some designers, television graphics has come to form part of our conception of television broadcasting. A brief survey of how the subject has been written about reveals a gap. Within the literature of graphic design, television graphics is considered a separate field; there are a few standard 'history of' books, usually written by past practitioners and rooted in an authorship perspective.[1] Although informative at one level, no analytical study is brought to bear on the subject by these texts. They offer descriptive surveys and unproblematized evolutions of style and technology peppered with individual heroes. The design press with startling regularity treat television graphics in terms of 'how it was done', as do the computer journals. It is obviously a generalization, but television graphics seem to lack a critical culture which other areas of design, to greater and lesser extents, enjoy.

Within Cultural and Media Studies there has been considerable critical attention given to television as a medium, as a technology and as an industry; in particular, work on genres such as news, soaps and sitcoms has been extensive. However, despite this impressive body of theoretical work, television graphics has been largely neglected.[2] Whether this is because it is perceived of as falling within the design discourse or as being inconsequential is hard to ascertain. The aim of this essay is to participate in bridging the divide by contributing to this early stage of critical thinking on the subject of television graphics. The focus will be to consider how television graphics 'work' by highlighting key debates regarding the televisual, technology and representation, with reference to contemporary (1993) television graphics in Britain.[3] The term 'television graphics' refers to an increasingly wide range of visual communication, and a surprising quantity of output across the four British terrestrial channels.[4] Put bluntly, television graphics occur at the beginning and end of programmes (titles and credits), during programmes (data, diagrams, animated sequences) and between programmes (continuity, identities, trailers and advertisements). The emphasis of this discussion will be on the continuity aspect of television graphics.

To date, graphics within programmes are used widely in certain genres such as sport, current affairs and 'youth' programmes, and are especially prominent in those which use a magazine format. They function in a variety of ways: shaping identity, marking-off sections within the televisual magazine, presenting statistical and other detailed information, changing the pace and adding humour. In sport, television graphics can help spectacularize programme content. This was particularly evident in the 1993 World Chess Championships televised on BBC and Channel 4, where they were a major factor in helping to transform this unlikely subject into acceptable television. In Channel 4's coverage, for example, the 'drama' and 'action' of the event was conveyed through simultaneously held windows showing a computer graphic of the chess board where 'next moves' were tested out visually, live action footage of the two figures of Kasparov and Short in head-on confrontation, and constantly updated numerical information on time used and moves made.

Title sequences are often discussed in terms of the programme content they 'package' – so acting as a taster of what is to come. This is rather simplistic.

BBC TV News   Copyright © BBC

Programme titles can work on different levels. For example, they may function generically; titles for an arts programme are recognizably different from titles for a game show. The titles introduced in 1993 for the BBC news at 9 o'clock exemplify a re-positioning of the programme from an individual identity, 'the 9 o'clock news' with its own distinctive titles, to a generic identity, 'the news' on BBC with the same titles as other news bulletins on the channel. The new identity privileges loyalty to the channel over loyalty to the programme.

It may be possible to argue that the television graphics which appear between programmes, in 'junctions', constitute a separate genre, with its own set of conventions. These very brief, intense graphics perform an important role in promoting the channels and their output. It may be convenient to think in terms of a division between graphics for channels (station identities) and for programmes (trailers, programme stills), but the situation is more complex; a whole range of categories to enhance programming is used. There are seasonal campaigns, usually five, such as 'Winter on One' and 'Christmas on Four' and holidays such as Bank Holiday and New Year's Day. There are also genres – comedy, drama, even hobbies such as gardening. Some genres are more generalized than others; the

Channel identity for BBC2

light entertainment identity on BBC1 can be used with a variety of individual programmes from games show to sitcom. Generic identities are also not rigidly applied; they may, like other identities, be used to create mood. Extended viewing hours have led to a day/night division, so, for example, ITV Meridian has 'Nighttime'. Increasingly we see examples of television channels devoting a period of time – an evening, a day, or a week – to a special theme as an overarching category, for example, Channel 4's 'Gimme Shelter', a week's programming about the homeless. Each of these ways of categorizing broadcast television is given visual and aural identity through television graphics in the form of identity sequences, trailers, menus and programme stills. The above is not an exhaustive list, but it begins to uncover the complex structures which inform promotion. It can be seen that the division between graphics for channels and for programmes is not a simple either/or. Channel identities will appear in logo form on graphics relating to an individual programme, or as a trailer for a series, and 'in jokes' such as the generic identities for BBC2 (drama – 2 in a doorway, documentary – 2 planing the floorboards) play on the channel identity, thus confusing their roles. The viewing conditions of television graphics further complicate the way in which they work. Typically they are seen in sequences. A characteristic sequence will involve a series of swift transitions, and might appear as: end of programme credits; identity for showcase series; trailer for programme within series; identity for showcase series close; next programme still; channel identity; ads; trailer for programme

71

Channel identity for BBC2

tomorrow (series); trailer for programme tomorrow (series); channel identity; programme titles.[5]

 Despite their importance, 'between programme' television graphics, unlike programme graphics, are not credited, nor do they appear in schedules printed in listings magazines such as *Radio Times* or in newspapers. This non-status reached a bizarre level with the BBC2 'Poems on the Box' initiative.[6] These 'programmes' consisted of short poems read by an off-screen voice with a stylish graphic treatment – an image of a bare room, moodily lit with a television flickering in the corner. Individual words and phrases from the spoken poem appeared on the screen with a sensitive typographic treatment. 'Poems on the Box' was a one week series, it had a strong identity and was trailed with two other programmes on the same one week theme of poetry. On the menu after the trailer, whilst these two other programmes were given allotted times, 'Poems on the Box' was actually listed as 'between programmes'. A curious phenomenon indeed – a programme which is not made conventionally visible, not even by the channel which is broadcasting it. Television graphics appears to be a defined, specific area, but as this brief survey indicates, it is highly complex and diverse.

The functioning of television graphics cannot be considered in isolation, it has to be seen within the context of broadcast output. Competition between channels means that capturing and keeping an audience is crucial. Television graphics play a key role in this, by sustaining what Raymond Williams has termed 'television flow'.[7] According to Williams, 'planned flow' is 'perhaps the defining characteristic of broadcasting'.[8] Although we like to think of television in terms of programmes, timed units with interruptions that we can look up and select, Williams argues that the experience of broadcast television is very different from this model, and that this is exemplified by the way in which we speak of 'watching television'. He suggests that sequences, not equivalent to programmes, compose the flow, and work to unify broadcast television, keeping the viewer hooked.

What is being offered is not, in older terms, a programme of discrete units with particular insertions, but a planned flow, in which the true series is not the published sequence of programme items but this sequence transformed by the inclusion of another kind of sequence, so that these sequences together compose the real flow, the real 'broadcasting'. Increasingly, in both commercial and public-service television, a further sequence was added: trailers of programmes to be shown at some later time or on some later day or, more itemised programme news...And with the eventual unification of these two or three sequences, a new kind of communication phenomenon has to be recognised.[9]

Williams's argument helps focus on the sequential organization of television graphics. Also, since 'Flow assembles disparate items, placing them within the same experience',[10] it helps us to think through the process by which television graphics, as distinct from filmic representation, are knitted into the televisual experience.

Consideration of the specificity of television graphics immediately raises the question of their difference as a form of representation. The majority of broadcasting television is 'realist', that is, it follows the conventions of realism by claiming to be 'the truth'. Most analytical work on television seeks to expose this apparent transparency of the medium, revealing it to be heavily constructed and ideologically loaded. It could be argued that the language of television graphics is quite different – it does not participate in the realist illusion. Television graphics are obviously constructed. The effect of realism is to ascribe to the television screen the role of 'window on the world' but in the case of television graphics, 'instead of looking through a transparent window to a world that lies beyond, con-tinuity sequences encourage the audience to observe the window itself, to look at it rather than through it.'[11] Imaging technology available today, however, has com-plicated this neat distinction. The BBC1 news developed in 1993 conforms to the accepted 'realist' image. We see a newsroom, lights, etc., but, with the exception of the newsreaders, everything in the image is assembled by a computer drawing on an image bank. It is a composite, generated image, but conceals its production. This kind of imaging presents an interesting philosophical question about the credibility of images produced differently but which carry the codes of previous technology such as photography, film and video.[12] Whether realist or not however, all television is constructed and has to be read; at its most basic, viewers have to make sense of the pattern of light energy on the screen.

Another important difference is that presentation graphics is often self-referential. As Morey points out, '…programme trailers, continuity announcements,

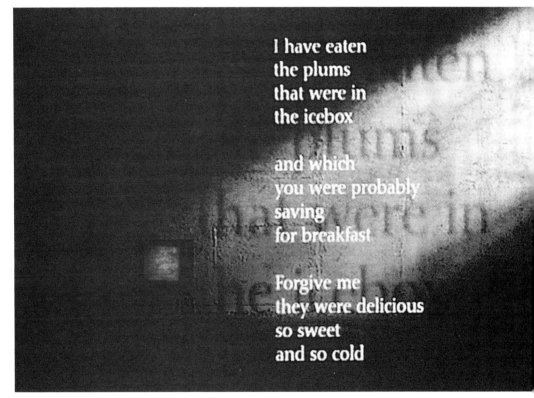

I have eaten
the plums
that were in
the icebox

and which
you were probably
saving
for breakfast

Forgive me
they were delicious
so sweet
and so cold

'Poems on the Box', BBC2

fault-apologies etc. compose a language of television talking about itself, a self-conscious, self-reflexive discourse'.[13] This can also extend to its own products; quotation and parody of previous television graphics forexample, is especially evident on Channel 4 and BBC2. As representations, television graphics can be marked out as different from 'the essentially nineteenth century technology of cinematographic film'[14] which dominates broadcasting. However it does not follow that they necessarily interrupt or disrupt television. On the contrary, as Williams's model of flow demonstrates, they unify broadcast output. Continuity of flow is partly maintained through sound. Most television graphics are accompanied by a voice over 'normalizing' what may be extravagant imagery.

Emphasis on the spoken word, some have argued, is a result of the development of the BBC from a producer of radio programmes.[15] Conventions of televisual language derive from previously existing technologies and media, despite the arguments to the contrary which state that it is a new 'pure' form. Clearly it 'borrows', for example, from graphic design tradition and animation conventions. Typography on television, though a moving image, is still firmly rooted in the conventions of print and book culture. Typefaces designed specifically for the screen are rarely used, and explorations of how typographic communication might work on screen – in space, over time, with sound – are very limited and marginalized. New forms and strategies for communication are emerging however. Programmes such as *Uncertainties* and *Small Objects of Desire* used television graphics predominantly to communicate programme content.[16] BBC1 has used a split screen device, condensing the image of the rolling credits of the outgoing programme and running the trailer for the next programme alongside it, simultaneously. This visual novelty was provoked by commercial considerations; the need to maintain the audience for the less popular programme which followed.

Technology is an important determining factor in televisual communication. For example the possibility of developing this device for holding several moving images on screen together is even more likely with the advent of High Definition Television. HDTV promises a new rectangular screen ratio of 16:9 (as opposed to 4:3) and increased visual resolution, 1050–1250 lines (as opposed to 525 or 625). However there is a danger of slipping into theoretical technological determinism. Historical examples have shown that it is not so much the potential of a technology, considered in isolation, but the ways in which it gets used which determine its influence. Tempting though it may be to speculate on the inherent qualities of HDTV and 'what it can do', this is unlikely to help define how televisual graphics of the twenty-first century will look, sound or function, since a whole set of determinants, social, economic and aesthetic will interact.

This essay was completed on 19 October 1993 during the time the above mentioned station identities were on the air.

74

It may be Wrapped but will it Warp?

Jon Wozencroft

It is too early to predict how, exactly, the conversion from analogue to digital forms will affect human communication and interaction on an everyday level. Already, it is possible to send computer files down a telephone line; we will soon all be able to publish our own faces on videophones hooked up to all corners of the globe; magazines with the wherewithal can retouch photographs to make smiles flash on full beam. Yet the full potential of new technology is still beyond our means; the cutting edge is never accessible, and by its very nature it never will be.

Fundamental changes in the process of transmitting language create fundamental changes in its expression. To have any chance of understanding the impact of digital forms of communication on the way we use language, we are, paradoxically when dealing with such a modern invention, forced to pretend that we are in a pre-condition rather than a 'post' state. The reduction of words and images to a system based on the binary code is not simply a sophisticated 'techno/logical development': it necessitates a revolution in the way we perceive any information.

In effect, we have two choices: to blindly go along with it, or to reconsider everything. And if we return to the origins of our language, to phonetics, hieroglyphs, embryo-writing and early alphabets, looking for clues or for archetypes of linguistic change, this is also a form of futurology, but retro-divination. There are drawbacks: we colour the past, lose sight of the present and fall subject to 'the disease of tomorrow'. And all the time we are compelled to weigh up whether or not anything is obvious anymore. Education systems are not working, every individual holds 'views' but few are in a position to make themselves heard, acronyms, euphemisms, jargon and catchphrases are used to such excess that a direct statement either leaves us speechless or is dismissed as another piece of advertising.

Having mastered the technique of building superstructures and shopping malls, we have forgotten how to build homes. So it is with language. In order to communicate, we designate our thoughts and feelings into prearranged compartments. To articulate means that we fill a space and hope to connect. We agree that an owl is not an elephant, but that is as far as it goes – in the main, we navigate a way through broad generalizations. Words, spoken in the first person, are primarily sonic devices with endless possibilities for personal pitch change – nuances and gestures that cannot be recorded on disk or tape even if they have been registered in real time.

The spoken word is standardized to keep pace with new modes of transmission. It becomes another format that can be captured in time and space; as Goebbels noted, 'the spoken word is more "magnetic" in its effect than the written one'. The chaos of communication has to be kept tidy, thus as soon as human encounters cease to be either original or impromptu (which is to say, relatively early on in the day), codes are developed to hold fast the compartments (here a parallel can be drawn with the fate of RMS *Titanic*). As the population and diversity of voices increases, so must the codes be made more rigid. Until communication, driven by mass media forms which expressly rely upon the concept of hidden (if not invisible) information, consists only of codes... then codes of codes of codes. Tabloidish, pastiche and self-referential terms become our staple diet – 'garbage in, garbage out', as the saying goes. And we shout to make ourselves heard.

In the best of all possible worlds, nothing needs to be recorded because the experience is always available. When a civilization devotes its energies to upholding (and thus redefining) its 'heritage' a storage problem arises – just like the housing crisis. As soon as the exposure and availability of any item or idea is restricted by the need to control the amount of people who wish to be exposed to it, the need to capture this information and to replicate it results. Words and ideas, like cities, become overpopulated. In this way, communication is no longer guided by the desire to emancipate, but the need to edit. The notion that, in today's marketplace, any product or message has to be 'commercial' in order to achieve 'a high profile' is often the kiss of death as far as meaning is concerned (and as for irony?!). This is the age of convenience, no matter what the cost. And the computer screen's *caveat emptor* – 'what you see is what you get' – legislates the illusion of substance, when any content can only be quantified in terms of *amount*.

Since different peoples evolve different solutions to their societies' needs for information storage, codes are as old as written language. In the beginning, everybody knew them – we presume. And if they did not, does this mean that language has always involved exclusion? Who knows? In spite of the fact that DNA research can now tell us more about the origins of man than ever before, we really have not got a clue. So rather than speculate, we can at least say that all forms of writing are a means of information storage. Anything stored needs to be codified. Is there an essential difference between early man, who made knots in a length of fabric as a mnemonic device, and modern man, who types letters on a keyboard and saves them on a hard disk?

As a noun, the first meaning of 'code' is a legal one. The word then develops to refer to a system or collection of rules of any sort. The lines you are now reading are, of course, in code, yet those of us who fall within the demographic range of the Roman alphabet and the English language have, from an early age, been instructed in its use and thus rarely inspect the cargo; its tradition as a common denominator determines that we would never consider it to be cryptic (from the Greek *kryptos*, 'secret'). Following this line, nor can Chinese/Arabic/Russian be

ATTRACTIVE, CARING FEMALE, 33, Virgin, seeks Messiah, 30 to 35, preferably outdoor type who likes to move mountains, for long and lasting relationship, possibly marriage. All letters answered with photo. Box 2001.

Insert for *Scanner 2*, © Touch 1993
Design: Jon Wozencroft, with thanks to John Critchley

assigned such a status, yet their alphabets are so unfamiliar to us that any written messages presented in these languages might as well be cryptographic.

At what point does a language become a code? Perhaps the dividing line is simply based on familiarity, and we have been misled by too many post-war spy films into thinking codes to be the privy of James Bond, Smiley's People, the government, the military and *The Prisoner*, and that to gain access to these codes would involve our crawling through a ventilation shaft, hoping that the guards will not be roused.

To press further for a distinction, the idea that all information in the public domain must be made familiar in style in order to appeal to a specific ('target') audience, and judicial, state and military information be encoded and 'made classified' creates a class system based on the relative ability of the reader or audience to receive and interpret the coded information. Codes are like camouflage: they are founded on the twin precepts of display and concealment. The distribution, the SEND, is all important. The method or process of disseminating information, the 'reaching out', the lying that is part and parcel of this process, demands that there be codes; and if this form of containment is insufficient, more direct forms of censorship can be called upon.

There is so much information vying for our attention that, inevitably, techniques are used to compress it into smaller loads, using codes to replace what may seem to be excess, complex or redundant wordage. This 'compression' is also regulated by time: deadlines, clearance, desk space, the available slot. The transmission of information must be made *efficient* to enable it to attract the right target audience. In the same breath, the world's information is increasingly articulated in one language – electronumerical US English (itself a hybrid) – so that every message becomes one that begs to be deciphered and then relocated and renewed using another code. Ours is a translation game.

The game has more losers than winners. The pressure of codification makes ('amateur') users of language turn (or retreat) to metaphors to 'fill out' and rebuild their flattened mental environment. The reduction of complex ideas to basic dimensions demands that we juggle signs around, twist them and redecorate. Then we wonder why and how we became confused.

The need to conceal and guard information is an ancient one. An early example AD is the so-called Caesar Alphabet, a basic method of transposing letters so that A becomes D and B translates to E. This, to be exact, is not a code but a cipher. A code works on complete words or phrases, and a cipher upon individual letters; there are two principal techniques – transposition and substitution. ('Cipher' comes from the Arabic *cifr*, meaning the arithmetical zero, and in this sense it has passed down into English to mean 'a mere nothing, a worthless person'). As for the word 'code', it now strikes us most often in its cybernetic sense (and is thereby better termed as a *formula*). This meaning did not enter the language until 1946. Accordingly, the noun merges with its verb. This linguistic shift is closely related to the progressive emphasis during the twentieth century on the use of codes in wartime – a hijack performed by the military. Just as Alan

Turing's improvised techniques cracked the German Enigma code, so was his later prototype for 'intelligent machines' adapted to compromise peacetime.

The very ability to mechanize message sending and receiving creates the capacity for 'Total War'. In turn, the possibility for artificial intelligence makes real life artificial. The apparent need now to define words in almost any context, from essays to ad campaigns to multimedia presentations, is proof enough that as far as our language is concerned, we are still in the dug-out.

5. *Cinemat. and Television.* The end of a session of filming or recording.

1974. M. AYRTON *Midas Consequence* 1. 63 Other cars are heard starting up out of shot and the lights on the pergola go off so I assume it's a wrap and the crew is listening to the director saying something consequential and busy about tomorrow's call. **1980** J. KRANTZ *Princess Daisy* xii. 191 'Right … it's a wrap.' … The large lights, cameras, sound equipment and other tools of the trade were quickly stowed away. **1983** *Listener* 23 June 18/2 The Director says: 'Cut! Thank you, Ben, that's a wrap – there is no more filming.'

Mapping Meanings

Visual Rhetoric and Semiotics

Edward Triggs

Persuasive messages are presented most often in the print media as a tripartite structure of picture, headline and text, visually unified through axial symmetry. This ubiquitous, easily identifiable form has prevailed for over a century and has become synonymous with messages intending to sell a product or service, or to propagandize a position on some issue. A questioning of this convention leads to an investigation of the system of rhetoric and the theory of semiotics. Presented here is a discussion of these concepts as they relate to the development of an alternative form, one which emerges organically when an argument the designer has determined is given visual form.

Introduction

Messages in the print media represent intentions and ideas through the selection and organization of visual elements known to or comprehend-ible to a reader. Some of these messages intend to inform, others to instruct, identify, entertain or persuade. Persuasive messages are those which intend to influence the purchase of a product or service, as in advertising, or to encourage acceptance of a position proffered on an issue or topic, as in propaganda.[1] Of concern here are those messages which intend to influence choice or redirect thought. An investigation of the rhetorical system and semiotic theory suggests an expanded role for the designer responsible for developing persuasive messages, and also, a way of actively engaging readers in the message. The art director/designer traditionally establishes a concept for a picture and determines appropriate typography for the headline and text. These three elements, picture, headline and text, are then organized into a conventional visual structure, usually symmetrical, which maintains the identity of each element. Rhetoric and semiotics provide an opportunity to forego the model of conventional form and allow form to grow organically as an effective integration of the visual and verbal languages which, as a unit, declares a graspable idea.

Rhetoric and its system

Rhetoric, simply defined, is the art of persuasion. Devised by the ancient Greeks and expanded into a system of interrelated activities by the Romans, rhetoric assists the development of a speech intended to persuade the listener to accept a position or opinion proffered by its speaker.[2] To be effective, Aristotle believed that a speech must appeal to the emotions of the listener, establish a favourable impression of the speaker's character, and prove the truth of statements made.[3] The speech, operating in a culture favouring ideas, oratory and aesthetics, had to exhibit a high degree of both intrinsic and extrinsic value through the choice of arguments, their organization and presentation. Although the classical system of rhetoric does not provide for the use of visual elements, selected concepts of the system can assist in making decisions affecting the structuring of ideas, choice of representational images and typeface – all of which determine a message's form and character. A speech unfolding over time allows the use of a host of rhetorical devices to argue its position and to establish a favourable character for the speaker. On the printed page where the 'speech' resides in its completeness as a tangible visual thing, the element of time is absent. The visually presented speech, as a graphic display, is an organic complex of inert words and pictures, colours and textures, whose meaning is dependent on the active participation of a reader. To achieve participation, the graphic display must first assert its presence and stimulate its reader to enter a mode of objective thought.

In his treatise on human knowledge, Karl Popper proposes that the human world is composed of three distinct, interrelated sub-worlds. The first world, 'the world of physical states', is where we speak of what we see; the second world, 'the world of mental states', is where we speak of our emotional reaction to what we observe; and in the third world, the world 'of ideas in the objective sense', we speak of the significance of what we have observed.[4] Following Popper's theory, we can say that identifying a thing as a message involves the first world; by enjoying the aesthetics of its visual form or being interested in what it says, we have brought the message into the second world. A message intended to persuade a reader to accept a new position on an issue cannot dwell in the emotional state of the second world, rather, it must be propelled into the third world where the idea it presents can be intellectually established, its value judged, and a decision made to agree with or reject the position proffered.

The ubiquitous tripartite form of picture–headline–text traditionally used to present persuasive messages in print is so familiar and easily identified as 'selling something' that its use as a triggering mechanism is counter-productive. What is needed to open the reader's third world is an accessible graphic display perceived as being a significant idea – an intelligible, objective thought. Using the concept of rhetoric, the designer is afforded an opportunity to establish a position or opinion of the content. It is in offering visual evidence to prove the designer's opinion that a non-traditional visual form will emerge.

Rhetorical arguments

A rhetorical argument used in speech or writing is a course of reasoning unfolding over time which intends to achieve agreement that a stated or implied proposition is true or accepted as being true. The components of an argument are most often based on premises acknowledged as being true, or on acceptable examples of similar cases.[5] In printed form, where the 'speech' is before the reader in its entirety, the rhetorical argument provides either a visual demonstration or visual evidence which proves the truth of an opinion the designer has of the proposition presented in the text. As an example: a proposition that a reader should send money to supply food for children starving in a certain country might lead the designer to establish an opinion that 'these children are vanishing'. Visual demonstration of the truth of this opinion might be a photograph of children evidencing malnutrition screened to about 40 per cent of black with text copy surprinted on the photograph.

Semiotics

Aristotle put forward the notion that each part of a natural thing has the potential of the complete thing of which it is part.[6] Relating his observation to printed communication, we can say that the recognition of a representation of a part of a thing points to the idea of the complete thing. A photograph of bark is both an imitation of natural bark and a suggestion of the complete tree.[7] This concept of a representation pointing to something other than itself is seen in the theory of semiotics, where a representation is not the physical thing itself but an indicator of ideas one might associate with that which is represented. Triggering awareness that an expression of a significant structured thought exists on the page is one of the aims of the designer being discussed. The reader must realize that a graspable, objective idea exists, one that is more than a description of things or a construction of persuasive utterances. Semiotics, being concerned with the relationship of things and meaning, provides assistance when selecting and configuring communication elements.

Semiotics is a broad, complex theory concerned with how meaning is attached to and derived from things in a given context.[8] The theory centres on the semiotic sign, a mental construction which arises when there is recognition of a correlation between an expression (signifier) and its content (signified).[9] For there to be a sign, someone must perceive an expression as referring to something other than itself. The recognition of something as standing for something else requires a stimulus external to the representation. The stimulus can be almost anything, such as one's desire to perceive things as signs, the context in which something appears, or the relationship one intended sign has to another. In the design of persuasive messages, it is the relationship between intended signs which activates 'sign-ness' and points to meaning. Signs, not being tangible objects *per se*, are suggested through the use of sign-vehicles, which have either a verbal form (words) or a non-verbal form (such as pictures, colours, arrows).[10] A pictorial sign-vehicle produced by photographic means is considered to be more immediately accessible to a reader than a representation produced by hand. Photographs have a desirable 'neutral rhetoric' as they continue to be perceived by the casual reader as representing a non-interpreted reality. Hand-constructed representations exhibit a value-laden rhetoric peculiar to the artist which impedes or redirects a reader from immediately perceiving what is denoted in its representation.

Traditional form

The role the art director/designer plays in preparing persuasive messages for the print media has changed little over the past 100 years, when advertising agents first employed artists to oversee the production of pictures and their addition to headlines and text. In this respect, the designer's involvement in the effectiveness of a message is limited to the creation of a visual rhetoric which projects value for the message and good character for its originator through the choice of typeface, colour and art direction of the photograph. All of this is done, of course, using the conventionalized message form of picture–headline–text. This familiar form becomes a message in itself which says, 'I am going to sell you something'. It is viewed here as being an obvious sign which often impedes or discourages reader participation. The alternative is a naturally derived form, one having a neutral rhetoric because the form develops organically from the selection, configuration and linking of elements necessary to present an argument established by the designer.[11] A neutral rhetoric is considered to exist when factors other than the argument are not an issue. This is similar to the concept of transparency and opacity in typography, where a word's visual form must not be so evident that access to its content is restricted.

The synthesis

Decisions affecting the selection, configuration and linking of sign-vehicles follow concepts offered in semiotics and rhetoric. Using the proposition given in the previous example, that children of a certain country are in need of monetary assistance, a photograph of children evidencing malnutrition is selected as the major element to demonstrate the designer's opinion that 'the children are vanishing'. The photograph represents 'real-ness', visible evidence of starving children, and from the rhetorical side, 'starving children' is an emotional appeal. The configuration of this pictorial image must be such that evidence of starvation and of children is immediately before the reader by removing all but essential information. The image must dominate the page, but not bleed off the page, as definition of the rectangular shape of a photograph assists in signalling 'sign'.[12]

Activating a sign

A sign is realized when activated by something other than itself. The fact that technology is used to reproduce a photograph on a page is not of sufficient importance to a casual reader to affect the switch from 'photograph' to 'sign'. Physically altering the image, such as screening it to 40 per cent of black, modifying its boundary or putting type on it, increases the chances of sign awareness on the part of the reader.[13] Colour also affects the perception of sign. In contrast to a full colour reproduction which reinforces the reality which existed in front of the lens, the translation of reality into black and white is a step away from 'real-ness' and a step toward 'sign-ness'. The reproduction of a photograph as a single colour halftone, say magenta, is an example of an undesirable rhetoric of aesthetics unless the colour chosen reinforces the argument (red for passion, green for coolness or envy, for example).

Visual syntax

The linking of sign-vehicles is a functional visual syntax which declares a conceptual structure, an idea, that is known or comprehensible to the reader. In rhetorical terms, the conceptual structure may be a demonstration, evidence, or a figure.[14] The rhetorical figure is 'an expression that is not ordinary and that has a form discernible by a particular structure', and, 'is argumentative if its use, leading to a change of perspective, seems normal in relation to the new situation thus suggested'.[15] In the context of the development of an alternative message form, a figure, visually presented, is considered as being 'not ordinary' as it is not part of the traditional picture–headline–text format. It is not ornamentation because it demonstrates the 'truth' of the argument determined by the designer. For purposes here, a visual rhetorical figure is anything perceivable as a structured idea. A diagram, sequence, substitution or repetition are examples of visual figures; simile, metaphor and paradox are linguistic structures.

Sign-vehicles

The figure determines the selection of sign-vehicles and their disposition, while recognition of the figure is the stimulus which activates the reader's world of objective thought. Each sign-vehicle must be arranged so as to reflect its contribution to the rhetorical figure. Analogy, being a comparison of two things, requires that sign-vehicles differ only in what they designate. The shape and size of each must be the same; the colour and texture, and the scale of the designated in each must also be similar. Metaphors, on the other hand, require differences in presentation. If a cheetah is used metaphorically to express the agility and speed of a sports car, the sign-vehicle of the cheetah must predominate while the object to which the idea of the cheetah applies (the car) must be presented in a smaller size. Each designated sign must retain its identity, therefore, the cheetah and the sports car cannot be present within the same sign-vehicle. As meaning is derived from the relationship of things designated, information other than that necessary to identify that designated must be eliminated from the sign-vehicle.

Argumentation

At least two sign-vehicles are required to present an argument. As a sign-vehicle can be presented verbally or pictorially, their combinations may be verbal and verbal, pictorial and pictorial, or verbal and pictorial. For example, a photographic image requires the presence of something else to activate awareness of a sign, and to establish the figure. That 'something else' may be a graphic device achieved through a technology, such as distortion, screening, or alteration of the natural colour of the represented; or a graphic sign, such as an X superimposed on the image, or a slicing apart and reorganization of the image. Two photographic images differing in what they designate, similarly configured and placed side by side, invite comparison (analogy); or, presented in different configurations and sizes invite a search for what is common in their apparent differences (metaphor or paradox). A verbal sign-vehicle composed of one or several words in display-size type purposefully juxtaposed with a pictorial sign-vehicle to create a rhetorical figure requires that its presence be equal to the presence of the pictorial to ensure that each vehicle is perceived as being a sign. The disposition of each sign-vehicle on the page must not be normal, rather, the positions must be other than ordinary, and be such that an interaction of their visual and conceptual aspects occurs.

Typography

Typefaces have a noticeable rhetorical effect on the character of a message. William Morris suggested the values of the Gothic period by selecting typefaces that evoked the sensation of being crafted by hand rather than faces which evidenced machine production. Bodoni before him paid tribute to the values of the classical period and those of his time when he designed a typeface to print papal missals. Historical typefaces are visual evidence of both the cultural values of their national origins and the level of technology existing at the time they were designed. Selection of a typeface based solely on historical references or designer preference is not desirable because it presents a too noticeable rhetoric which impedes immediate access to the argument presented. The appropriate typeface for use in the alternative message form under discussion is one whose texture is in visual agreement with the visual texture of the photograph and the conceptual texture of the argument. If an argument concerns 'conflict', an aggressive typographic texture is required; conversely, the concept of 'grace' would be enhanced through the use of a typeface which produces a quiet, fluid texture.

Summary

The role traditionally assigned the designer of persuasive messages presented in the print media is one of establishing an effective visual rhetoric through art direction or a representational image and selection of appropriate typography. The rarely questioned traditional form of the message, that of a picture–headline–text, continues to be identified as a message that attempts to sell something. Judicious application of selected concepts of rhetoric and semiotics is an effective means of determining new forms unrestricted by allegiance to conventional models; that is, a form which arises naturally from an argument the designer has developed as a persuasive entry point for reading of the text.

The London Underground Diagram

John A. Walker

There are a number of reasons for choosing a diagram as a subject for analysis: diagrams employ a variety of means to encode information; the signs they contain are intentional and clearly presented; therefore, diagrams are relatively simple to decipher in comparison with paintings, for example. In a diagram, the functional features of the image can be readily distinguished from the non-functional, whereas in a painting this may not be such a straightforward task. When a viewer studies a modern painting they may have difficulty in deciding whether scratches in the paint surface were made by the artist or whether they are accidental additions.

A valuable characteristic of objective human knowledge (objective in the sense that it exists in the public domain) is that macrocosmic systems which are only fully comprehended by a few specialists are made known to ordinary citizens by means of microcosmic models. This feature of knowledge, so familiar that it is taken utterly for granted, is exemplified by the London Underground Diagram, (henceforward 'LUD'), a two-dimensional model which, through the agency of reproduction, is made available to the general public for consultation at any point both within and without the London Underground railway network (the macro-cosm). Millions of travellers make use of the LUD millions of times every week, yet no one appears to pay it any special attention: passengers look *through* it rather than at it. Although this indifference can be interpreted as a tribute to the superlative functionalism of its design, one might have expected some sign of appreciation from British art critics since most of them reside in London and the diagram is, arguably, a masterpiece of twentieth-century graphic art. Until now the only substantial article on the LUD and its designer Henry C. Beck (1901–74) is a factual account of its development by the graphic artist Ken Garland.[1]

The Underground *diagram* is also commonly referred to as an Underground *map* but the former lacks certain features typical of maps (though, as we shall see later, diagrams and maps do share some characteristics). In order to elucidate the distinction between diagram and map, it is necessary to state some obvious features of maps: most maps are graphic representations of the whole, or part, of the earth's surface. They reduce a three-dimensional world to a two-dimensional plane. Because they depict curved surfaces on flat pieces of paper, distortions occur, and because the size of each piece of paper is much smaller than the size of the area it maps, there are great reductions of scale. In spite of their distortions, maps exhibit a high degree of isomorphism with the areas they represent

The London Underground Diagram

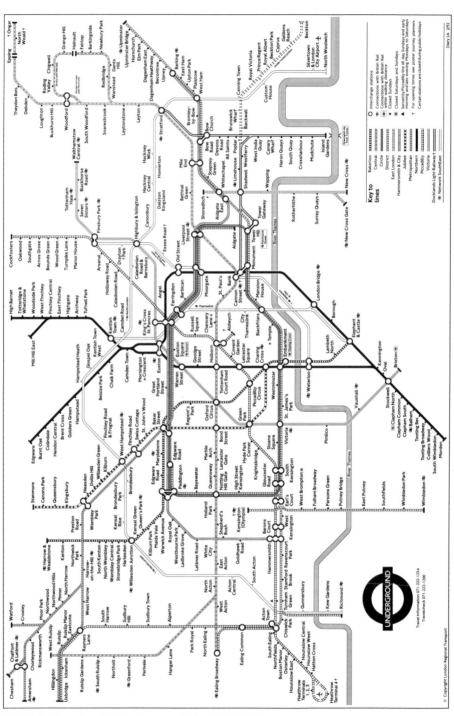

Paul E. Garbutt: London Underground Map (93/1938)

graphically: if an accurate map of a relatively small flat region of the earth were enlarged until it was equal in size to that region, then it would fit over it exactly. Such is not the case with the LUD: if enlarged to the actual size of London it would diverge markedly from the geography of the terrain for the simple reason that it is a highly schematic representation of the Underground system and furthermore, unlike a map, it is not drawn to scale. These aspects of the diagram can mislead passengers who try to use it as a guide to the location of surface features or to the actual distances between stations; they soon discover how approximate the diagram is in relation to the actual surface topography of London. The radical difference between map and diagram can be seen at a glance if the first route guide to the Underground – a map designed by F. H. Stingmore in use from 1919 to 1933 – is compared to Beck's design.

89

Beck conceived the idea of the diagram in 1931 and though it was originally rejected as 'too revolutionary', it replaced Stingmore's map in 1933. From 1933 to 1959 Beck was responsible for the design of the diagram and its numerous revised editions. The current diagram, designed by Paul E. Garbutt, is heavily indebted to Beck's classic design and London Transport ought to acknowledge this fact by printing a credit to Beck on the diagram. Revisions of the LUD were (and still are) necessitated by the opening of new tube lines, but new versions were also produced in order to incorporate additional information suggested by staff or members of the general public. Many revised versions were abandoned as failures because the 'improvements' tended to over-complicate the design.

Beck was by profession a draughtsman, and it was during a period of unemployment, after having been made redundant by London Transport, that it occurred to him that he could 'tidy-up' the old 'Vermicelli' map of Stingmore's 'by straightening the lines, experimenting with diagonals and evenning out the distances between stations'.[2] As Garland has pointed out, Beck's three most significant innovations in 1931 were: the substitution of diagram for map; a restriction to three directions of lines (horizontal, vertical and diagonal) and enlargement of the central area. The design problem which prompted these innovations was that of accommodating within a limited rectangular space all the lines radiating towards the outlying districts of London and, at the same time, maintaining clarity in the overcrowded centre. The problem was aggravated every time a new tube line was introduced. Beck realized that clarity and geographical truth were antithetical to one another and that geographical accuracy had to be abandoned in favour of clarity. In other words, Beck's choice of diagram rather than map was the result of an evaluation of different modes of representation in relation to the needs of the travelling public. There is a general lesson here: no representation tells the whole truth about reality, every representation is partial and selective in what it depicts; every picture conceals as much as it reveals. Consequently, an artist's choice of representation must be based on what he or she considers are in the best interests of those they have chosen to serve. Before consideration can be given to the pictorial conventions and coding mechanisms of the LUD it is necessary to tabulate its components:

The London Underground Diagram

Network

The diagram consists of a number of lines converging towards a central core delimited by the Circle Line. The lines intersect at various points to form a network structure. To ensure clarity this network is inscribed on a uniformly white background.

Background

The rectangular poster is displayed vertically like a painting but, unlike a picture, its four dimensions have directional properties, that is, top/bottom and left/right are implicitly understood by the viewer to represent north/south and east/west. In one version of the diagram, a north-pointing arrow was introduced but it was quickly realized that this symbol was redundant.

Border

Most large posters of the diagram have borders consisting of a thick blue line, while diagrams printed as pocket-sized folders have borders consisting of a narrow black or blue line.

Grid

The background of the current diagram is divided into squares by a co-ordinate grid, which, when used in association with a list of station names, enables strangers to London to pinpoint the location of stations on the diagram.

Colour

Each tube line is assigned a distinctive colour which enables them to be easily distinguished and memorized. Names and colour codes of all the lines are given in a key contained in a box placed in a corner of the diagram. At one stage the coloured lines also incorporated the names in printed form but this awkward piece of design contradicted the colour coding system. It did have one advantage; when the diagram was printed in black and white, the lines could still be identified.

River

The only surface feature represented on the LUD is the River Thames which is depicted by means of a blue band. This band includes the words 'River Thames' and it narrows progressively from right to left to indicate downriver–upstream. As a result of the process of geometricization, the natural undulations of the Thames have virtually disappeared in the graphic symbol. Another alteration is that the tube lines which pass under the river are printed over it in the diagram.

Stations

These are indicated by square ticks on the lines and by circles, some of which are interlinked to indicate interchange stations.

The London Underground Diagram

Language

The diagram contains a number of words and phrases: names of stations and lines; explanatory statements; the title of the diagram and the name of the designer.

Miscellaneous symbols

These include a zig-zag line to show an escalator connection; the logo of British Rail to indicate Underground stations which link up with British Rail stations; red crosses and stars to indicate stations whose opening hours are different from the rest; a plan view of an aircraft to indicate Heathrow Airport and a circle intersected by a horizontal bar – the symbol of London Transport.

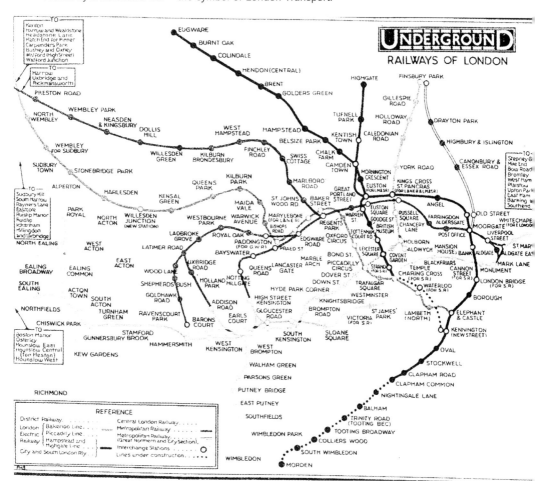

F. H. Stingmore: the first route guide to London Underground, in use from 1919–33

It has already been established that the LUD does not represent its object in the manner that maps normally do, but none the less the diagram is, to a degree, an iconic representation of the Underground system. Charles Morris remarks, 'a sign is iconic to the extent to which it itself has the properties of its denotata'; and since both the diagram and the Underground system are networks of lines, the first is, in this respect, an icon of the second.[3] Essentially, the diagram depicts a set of points and the way they are joined up. In the terminology of graph theory it is a 'finite connected graph'. Consequently, it reproduces precisely those properties of the Underground system which are of most significance to the traveller and ignores those which are of little significance. Network analysis is now a commonplace technique of business management. Its purpose is to solve network routing problems by finding the optimum paths between nodes in relation to such factors as time, distance and cost. Every time travellers on the Underground use the diagram to work out the best and cheapest route from starting point to destination they are unwittingly solving a network routing problem. The value of the diagram is that it makes it possible for travellers to journey to their destination in logical space, by alternative routes if necessary, before committing themselves to travelling in physical space. Leonard Penrice points out that in making railway journeys travellers 'play a kind of game according to certain rules. They start and finish journeys at stations; they count, and recognize the name of, stations they go through; and they change from one line to another at certain points'.[4] Penrice argues that Beck's achievement was to design a diagram 'on which an identical game could be played according to essentially similar rules'. The relation between railway and diagram is not, according to Penrice, a static resemblance such as one finds in a photograph: the diagram and the traveller 'together constitute a kind of working model of the railway, and not a static representation'.

All copies of the LUD inside the Underground system represent their own location (this is one characteristic which the LUD shares with maps). Charles Sanders Peirce explains, 'on a map of an island laid down upon the soil of that island there must, under all ordinary circumstances be some position, some point, marked or not, that represents *qua* place on the map, the very same point *qua* place on the island'.[5] Thus once we are inside the Underground our position is always locatable on the diagram. When we consult it on a station platform, our first task is to establish our position in relation to the rest of the network. At one time, diagrams contained an arrow and the phrase 'you are here' to single out the station in question.

As a sign, the directional character of the rectangular ground is purely conventional: the diagram as a stimulus object does not contain any symbol indicating the fact that its top edge is 'north'. This property is imputed to the diagram by the traveller whose interpretation of the diagram is governed by the context of transportation and general knowledge concerning the convention of map reading. In an art gallery the 'same' rectangular ground would invoke a different set of conventions.

In logic, the purpose of a linear enclosure, and in art, the purpose of a frame, border or mount, is to establish the boundary of a particular universe of discourse, to isolate a domain from the flux of experience. But since the edges of the poster literally demarcate the limits of the domain, the presence of a graphic border in the LUD might seem an unnecessary move on the part of its designers. However, by repeating graphically the rectangular shape of its support, the border emphasizes that the domain it encloses is a metaphorical one, not a literal one.

Just as the diagram functions as a key or index to the Underground system, the grid used for locating stations and the box explaining the colour coding operate as keys to the diagram. They are signs within a sign. Clearly the grid does not denote anything exterior to the diagram; it merely divides the ground into equal segments. Cross-referencing is achieved by the combination of two arbitrary

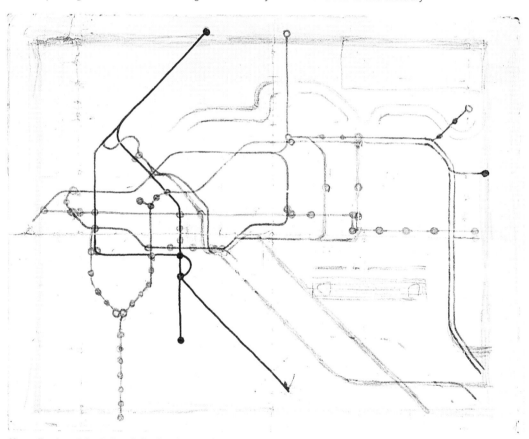

Harry Beck: original sketch for London Underground, 1931

codes: the alphabetic and the numerical. These devices are printed along the vertical and horizontal axes of the grid. Since the key to the diagram is a meta-sign (a sign about a sign), the purpose of the frame which encloses it is, like quotation marks in a conventional text, to mark the boundary between object-sign and meta-sign, so that the viewer does not confuse the two in reading the diagram.

While the colour coding of the lines is totally arbitrary and monosemic (in the LUD 'yellow' has no meaning apart from 'Circle Line'), it is inevitable that for regular travellers the colours will acquire connotative meanings apart from their denotative ones. The emotional associations developed in response to the colours of the line will vary from person to person; their potential for meaning is infinite. However, the sense of inappropriateness which most Londoners feel when they learn that the red Central Line was once orange in colour demonstrates how closely each line becomes identified in our minds with its tincture. Exceptionally, the hue of the Central Line does seem to extend beyond the realm of the arbitrary in that this line is compositionally one of the most important, since it functions as the baseline or spine for the rest of the network. Its structural importance is sig-nalled by the fact that it is assigned the most dynamic colour in the spectrum.

94

Turning now to the representation of the River Thames, water is naturally colourless but according to the conventions of map-making, it is always blue. At first sight this seems a purely arbitrary coding, but it is in fact 'relatively moti-vated' (to use Saussure's terminology), that is, on cloudless days water is blue. Furthermore, blue is generally experienced as a 'cool' colour; therefore it signifies the coldness of water. The narrowing of the graphic river from right to left indi-cates, of course, the narrowing of the river which occurs from east to west.

Of great importance is the fact that the meaning of the graphic image is mediated linguistically. Imagine the diagram bereft of all names of stations and lines and without the explanation given in the key. It would still display the structure of the Underground system but its effectiveness as a guide would be nullified. However, as Roland Barthes has pointed out, one of the chief functions of linguistic elements accompanying images is to anchor their meaning.6 Without a title on the LUD, a stranger to London would not know what system the diagram represented.

Subsidiary signs found within the diagram, such as the logos of London Transport and British Rail, are symbols (according to Peirce's triad of signs: index/icon/symbol); that is, conventional signs standing for large scale transporta-tion enterprises. On the other hand, considered in isolation, each logo has iconic features; for example, the two horizontal lines in the British Rail logo obviously represent railway lines. The iconic features of the London Transport logo are more problematic. Various interpretations of it have been offered. One example is that it represents London (the circle) and London Transport's ability to cross the city (the horizontal bar). The London Transport logo reminds us that the LUD is but a sin-gle unit in a much larger system of signs encompassing the whole of London's tubes and buses. Taking a narrower view, it can be readily appreciated that the LUD is the 'mother' of a whole series of route diagrams depicting parts of the net-work, that is, those displayed in station passageways and inside tube trains.

In addition to its denotation 'Underground system', the LUD has acquired a supplementary signification in the years since it was introduced: as a decorative motif on gifts and souvenirs produced for tourists, the diagram functions, like the images of St Paul's, the Tower and the Houses of Parliament, as a symbol for London. Since the LUD was consciously composed, it necessarily signifies a set of aesthetic values, in this instance, certain principles of design historically associated with Classicism; namely, order, unity, harmony, stability, purity, clarity, economy, anonymity of finish and rationality. These values are not communicated via symbols; on the contrary, they are signalled by the perceptual characteristics of the sign vehicles themselves. For example, the impression of clarity is achieved by the use of lines with hard rather than blurred edges and by the use of a range of colours which are highly differentiated from one another. Similarly, the impression of purity is achieved by the use of saturated hues.

In conclusion, a few remarks about the utility value of the LUD. Frank Pick, for many years an administrator for London Transport, dedicated himself to

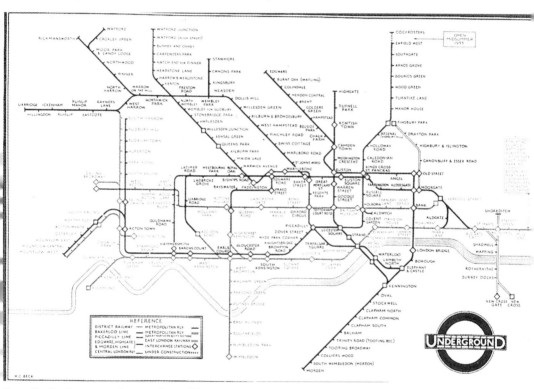

Harry Beck: diagrammatic map, first edition, 1933

improving the quality of design for the London commuter by commissioning leading modern architects to build new stations and leading graphic designers to produce typography and posters for the Underground. Beck's diagram was not commissioned by Pick, it was a lucky bonus which matched the philosophy of utilitarianism – Bentham's concept of the greatest happiness for the greatest number – which I take to be the ideology of the London Transport executive in the 1930s. Utilitarianism can be criticized on the grounds that it permits dictatorship – providing it is benevolent – and perhaps today a designer would feel it necessary to encourage public participation in the decision making process leading to a design solution, rather than merely producing a design on the public's behalf, without any consultation.

Marx claims in *Das Kapital* that 'the utility of a thing makes it a use-value'. Things which have use-value for others besides the person who made them have social use-value. However, the fact that the LUD has social use-value does not mean that it escapes being a commodity. Clearly the original design which Beck produced while employed as a wage labourer by London Transport could now be sold as a commodity, but even the copies of the diagram given away 'free' by London Transport are commodities: they have no use-value except for those travelling via the Underground and this service costs money, therefore the use of the diagram is included in the price of tickets.

What is important about the LUD is that it is a sign of exceptional richness and social utility. It is a work of graphic design which literally works every day, and evolves year by year to meet changing circumstance. Hence, it provides a model for the role of art in a future society. Designers generally tackle specific problems which are set by others, consequently they rarely have the opportunity to question the broader context within which the design problems are posed. This is the factor which limits the usefulness of the LUD as a model for current art practice.

This article is reprinted from *Icographic* 14/15 (1979) with special thanks to the International Council of Graphic Design Associations (ICOGRADA).

Poliscar

Krzysztof Wodiczko

The name of the vehicle, Poliscar, comes from the same root as police, policy and politics, namely the Greek word for city-state, *polis*. In ancient Greece the word referred more to a state of society characterized by a sense of community and participation of the citizen (*polites*) than to an institution or a place. To be a citizen is by definition to be a legitimate and protected member or inhabitant of the community and as such, entitled to the rights and privileges of a 'freeman'. The Poliscar is meant both to underscore the exclusion of the homeless from the city community and to provide them with some means of participating in it.

The homeless population is the true public of the city in that they literally live on the street, spending their days and nights moving through the city, working and resting in public parks and squares. The contradiction of their existence, however, is that while they are physically confined to public spaces, they are politically excluded from public space constitutionally guaranteed as a space for communication. They have been expelled from society into public space but they are confined to living within it as silent, voiceless actors. They are in the world but at the same time they are outside of it, literally and metaphorically. The homeless are both externalized and infantilized and as externalities and infants they have neither a vote nor a voice. As long as the voiceless occupy public space, rendering them their voice is the only way to make it truly public.

The Poliscar is designed for a particular group of homeless persons, those who have communications skills and the motivation to work with the homeless population in organizing and operating the Homeless Communication Network, an important part of which will be the fleet of mobile communications and living units – the Poliscars. The vehicle will respond to some of the most urgent communication needs of the different groups within the homeless population. It will be serving mostly those who live on the streets and in empty lots, helping them learn and expand communicative strategies and technologies. Some of these are already well developed by the homeless who inhabit abandoned buildings – the squatters. It will establish links between various encampments, forming new social ties and leading to greater intercommunity and urban organization for this emerging constituency.

Through the Homeless Communication Network and its equipment the Poliscar will

a. increase the sense of security among those who live outside by transmitting emergency information, such as early warning of planned evictions and other dangers facing both the homeless and non-homeless in troubled areas. Its use can help them organize quick and massive social action in the face of impending threats. In this way the position of the homeless living in empty lots will be closer to that of squatters who are already developing telecommunications systems for the same purpose.

b. help develop forms of communication necessary for the participation of home-less populations in municipal, state and federal elections. The Homeless Communication Network and Poliscars will provide a medium for articulation, exchange and confrontation of ideas, opinions, experiences, visions and expres-sions among different groups in the homeless population. Concurrently, it can take advantage of material and information transmitted from other networks.

c. develop a sense of social and cultural bonds among the members of the groups. This implies an increased understanding of antagonisms and differences, resulting in a decrease of tensions and feelings of alienation of one homeless group or individual from another. At the same time, the preconceived, fixed and a priori image of the homeless population and its identity produced and reproduced by existing official networks of communication will be challenged by this experi-mental speech-act machine for homeless self-representation and expression.

d. help create and record not only images but also individual histories of the homeless. History in this context means the relationship between the present situ-ation and the changing city, and the changing life of that person within it. Democracy, liberty and identity are all forms of continuing practice that cannot be separated from the instances of their expression, communication and, by implica-tion, reception by the larger population.

e. produce both image and sound programmes which could aid different groups and individuals to considerably extend and expand existing action groups' con-stituencies and constantly update the information in professional areas such as:

1. legal aid – listings and interactive forums for issues within the realm of the law.
2. medical aid – health and drug advice.
3. social crisis aid – helping people to communicate with one another in critical situations, taking into account the specificity of their life on the streets, encamp-ments and squats through counselling by homeless and non-homeless psycho-logists, sociologists, etc.
4. expression and individual histories.
5. formulation of political, educational and aesthetic strategies.

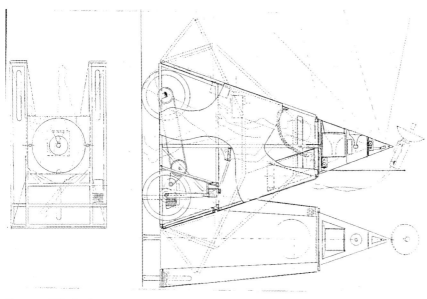

Krzysztof Wodiczko: computer-generated drawing for Poliscar , c. 1990–1

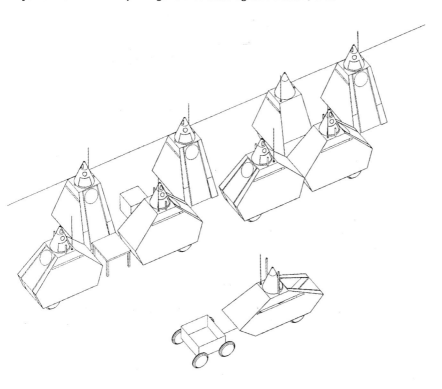

Krzysztof Wodiczko: computer-generated drawing for Poliscar, c. 1990–1

f. help the economic system of the homeless population enter the larger economic system of the city. There is a possibility of advertising available skills and commodities and using the communication system for job listings within certain labour markets. Employers who wish to employ homeless people could use the network as a database as well as advertising for their own needs. Events (fairs, theatrical and musical performances, etc.) could be listed as either public or private listings. The homeless are treated, at best tolerated, as aliens on their own planet. This 'alienation' – making into legal aliens legitimate operators within today's city – has the vicious effect of excluding not only the homeless, but us – the 'community' –

Krzysztof Wodiczko: Poliscar, 1991, walking position

from those real masses of 'strangers' from whom we are estranged and with whom we presume to have no common language. In fact it is the strangeness of the situation that we project on to others rather than confronting it together.

This contradiction – to us they may seem strange in the city, but are not strangers to the city – results in a contradictory and complex identity: the savage homeless in a noble city, or the noble homeless in a savage city. Squeezed between this play of images, the homeless themselves, in their complexity in a complex city, remain out of the picture, which has no room for the real life of people for whom it happens to lack a dwelling.

Krzysztof Wodiczko: Poliscar in New York

Fashion Follows Form

Steven Heller

Drugs and rock-and-roll inspired the 1960s psychedelic poster in the same way that computer and video inspired 1980s multi-layered typography. Both altered conventions that had held sway since the Second World War and pushed standards of perception codified by the Moderns. Both have been accepted by dedicated audiences for whom such codes are easily decipherable. Both have made such an impact on the field that historians of graphic design cannot help but cite these approaches as being of their times. Yet, both have also invited criticism. It's an old story, really. New media plus new ideas plus new passions equals new paradigms, and new paradigms foster reaction. But despite the antagonism, history proves that some of the most difficult experiments and egregious errors have resulted in important new developments in art and design.

The psychedelic poster, for example, was born into a period of social and cultural flux. Its pioneers chose to violate accepted practice in order to communicate with an audience that was already being exposed to new stimulants. Initially the flea market graphic sensibility employed to advertise music concerts merely echoed the trappings of the San Francisco hippy and rock scene, but a language soon developed as the artists began to pull and tug around the edges. In its early stage, around 1967, a raw and untutored psychedelic style was created by comic strip and hot rod artists who followed their instincts. In its accelerated mature phase, a year later, one of its outstanding proponents, Victor Moscoso, deliberately reversed the canonical rules about harmony and balance that were developed by the Moderns and were dominant at the time. Moscoso, who had studied at Yale with Josef Albers, believed that unadorned Modern design would have little impact on the new generation, and so transformed its taboos into new standards. Vibrating colours and negative spaced type made posters much harder to read, but Moscoso correctly reasoned that the audience was willing to make the sacrifice in return for the payoff.

The payoff was a visual language all their own.

Deconstructivist typography, an umbrella term inspired by linguistic theory and signified by the layered look, had a more complicated birth and various midwives. During the 1970s, Basel designer Wolfgang Weingart developed a system of typographic order as an alternative to the dominant Neue Grafik or International Style. On the surface, this new approach was chaotic, yet underneath it was built on a structure of hierarchical logic. Many of Weingart's followers had been schooled in Modern academies and found that his new method released them from old strictures. The Modern canon was already becoming increasingly anachronistic as shifts in technology, economy and politics began to unhinge the canonical absolutes.

Electronic media and computer technology were beginning to suggest, if not define, new ways to present information. With new media, visual communications could no longer afford to be one-dimensional. As the traditional methods of designing books and magazines were challenged, visionary American designers like April Greiman and Dan Friedman began experimenting with new ways of

Victor Moscoso: © 1967 Neon Rose

busting the grid. Harnessing the primitive characteristics of electronic media and making strengths out of technological weakness resulted in a new method that evolved over time into a language. Multiple layers of discordant types and integrated images became a commentary on the information deluge on the one hand, and a signpost for new reading and viewing pathways on the other. In fact, this discordancy was not unlike the typography of the late 1890s, the nascent and chaotic period of commercial design, when job printers randomly mixed different types for fashion and function. So, the 'new wave' appropriately underscored yet another state of cultural and aesthetic flux.

Deconstructivism was promoted in various academies where a hothouse

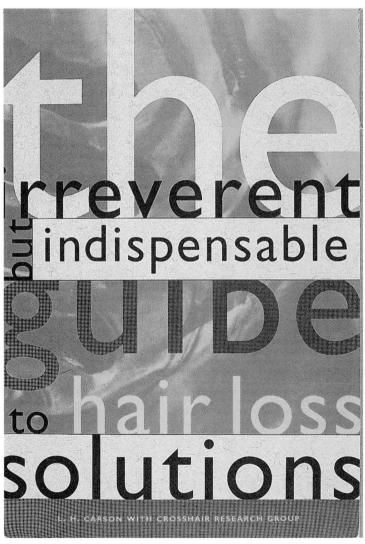

Book jacket by Tara Carson, reproduced by kind courtesy of the artist

sensibility was, in part, bolstered by linguistic theory. Graduate schools encouraged testing limits free from the outside rigours imposed by the requisites of business. In a relentlessly free atmosphere, students explored the fringes of communication with the hope of making discoveries that would exorcize the *status quo*. Yet it is not possible to gauge effectiveness by laboratory projects alone, but rather by how the discoveries survive and function in the real world.

In 1983, one year before the introduction of the Macintosh computer, Rudy Vanderlans and Zuzana Licko founded an alternative culture magazine called *Emigre*. What began as the cousin of a 1960s era underground newspaper soon developed into the clarion of digital typography and design. The first Macintosh

Emigre, Number 19

and its primitive default faces inspired *Emigre*'s parents to focus on design as, Vanderlans has called it, 'a cultural force'. So, rather than being a passive cultural observer, *Emigre* became a pioneer in typeface design, one of the most significant developments in the PC era. In addition to developing many of the earliest dot-matrix and later, as the technology improved, high resolution typefaces, *Emigre* showcased the leading proponents of a new typography who were at once the scions and the rebels of Swiss and American 'new wave' design. Like psychedelicists, the designers promoted through *Emigre* sought to reach audiences that were uninterested in, and perhaps turned off by, Modern approaches, and so developed visual codes that forced new reading and viewing habits.

These new approaches were welcomed by some, but considered a 'red flag' by others. Once released from the relative safety of the laboratory, the tension between old and new ignited. While progress in art and design is inevitable, the baton is never passed as smoothly as one might hope. Old assumptions are rarely relegated to the junk heap without resistance. Yet action and re-action in design are as natural as the changing tides and just as necessary. As the arguments force practitioners of all ages to assess and defend their positions, stasis, the hobgoblin of creativity, is disrupted. Although short-lived, psychedelia was important because it thoroughly challenged stasis and exposed anachronism, forcing practitioners to question deep-seated beliefs about beauty, functionality and appropriateness. Deconstructive approaches likewise encouraged a re-evaluation of old methods and aesthetics in the light of a new technological era. Both methodologies became milestones for their respective eras and touchstones for progress but, and here is the inevitable paradox, they also became templates for mimicry.

It is axiomatic that when a method or manner enjoys too much popularity, indeed when it becomes formulaic, its edges are smoother and its teeth are dulled. By the time the avant-garde enters the mass consciousness, many of its successful experiments have been diluted and have become little more than style. In fine art, the acceptance of radical approaches into the mainstream may mean victory for its proponents, but ultimately, the most progressive forms have been neutered, if not trivialized, to appeal to a widespread audience. When Abstract Expressionism was embraced by the American art establishment in the 1950s, it lost much of its stridency and soon devolved into the official art of corporate culture. In design the same can be said of the Modern movement; born of radical ideals during the 1920s, Modernism evolved in the post-war period into a sanitized International Style, which was also embraced by corporate culture. It is ironic that the goal of the twentieth-century artist is to discover new territory – and stay, at least precariously, on the edge – yet what artist does not hope that their discovery *will* be recognized and accepted by patrons, if not the culture itself. In graphic design, being an outsider is even more of a contradiction. The commercial nature of design necessitates that what is outside either be brought inside or be deemed irrelevant. Regardless of how strong or determined the proponents of Psychedelia and Deconstruction were to forge new directions, they were incapable of preventing the appropriation of their language.

Psychedelia was on the fringe only for a short time before the synthesizers and assimilators began making the black-light monstrosities that today typifies psychedelia in the public's nostalgic mind. The cultural feeding frenzy that overtook the 'youth culture' was predictable, and yet the hardcore hippies attempted to ward off trivialization when they symbolically acknowledged the death of their 'movement' in a mock funeral in San Francisco's People's Park less than two years after it began. Although the trappings of hippydom continued for several more years, all that remained of the psychedelic posters after 1968 were the stylistic affectations applied to a wide range of mainstream and faux youth culture products.

Deconstructivist typography has been incorporated into a variety of design programmes at various colleges, and is proffered through the work of various practitioners. Since it is not identified exclusively with a marketable and exploitable youth culture as was Psychedelia, Deconstructive typography has not been as thoroughly co-opted by the entrepreneurs. But it has proliferated and transformed beyond its experimental stage into the mainstream as a 'cool' or 'hip' way to communicate, and now is featured on books, magazines and TV commercials. In this sense it has become a mannerism that is often inappropriately applied in knee-jerk fashion.

That is the nature of fashion follows form.

Deconstructivist typography is, in its variegated iterations, no different than any other cultural jargon, visual or otherwise. When used as a code, it effectively cues the reader and viewer as it demarcates a cultural territory. But as a mannerism it becomes a silly conceit as ridiculous as OpArt during the late 1960s or as quaint as faux-Constructivist typography a few years ago. In its pure forms – the way *Emigre* and the new rock magazine, *Ray Gun*, present it – ongoing experimentation tests the boundaries of art and commerce. In its diluted form, the quality of the original succumbs to the thoughtlessness of the acolytes. Although it is impossible to legislate as to how an offspring develops, designers must nevertheless recognize the consequences that result when style overtakes substance, and perhaps restrain themselves from contributing to the redundancy and irrelevancy that inevitably diminishes graphic design.

Design, Communication and the Functioning Aesthetic

David Rowsell

Imagine you are fortunate enough to be shown an example of graphic design produced by an alien being. As with most science fiction aliens, this one shares many physical features with humans, so we are in no doubt as to what it is we are examining. Given that the object of our gaze is a design, we could probably make some intelligent guesses as to what the design is about; it might resemble Earth designs of a particular type, and so on. However, as yet we are unable to speak 'Alien' so can say little specific on the subject of what the design communicates. We can only guess at its meaning to a native speaker of 'Alien' who can be said to know the meaning. Alien linguistic marks are different to any written Earth language and we fail in our attempts to make sense of them. What remains, then, is a design without communication. No clear message is conveyed until such time as we learn the 'Alien' language. Still, we might amuse ourselves for a while by examining the design from a purely formal point of view – as a collection of marks and colours. This formal residue may be pleasing or not. Either way, there is enough for us to respond to the look of the design. It could evoke all manner of thoughts or responses in us, to the point where we become imaginatively engaged in the design. In short, the alien design, devoid of linguistic meaning, seems to become an aesthetic object – just like a work of art.

Let us suppose that the imagined design looks good; we find it appealing and to our taste. Perhaps we want to talk about the harmonious balance of black marks against white, or the way in which the colours complement each other. With such observations and responses we very easily enter into a critical debate about the aesthetic merits of a particular design. If we contemplate our imagined object for a moment longer, and continue to feel that it happens to look good, then we may well wonder why this is so. It is probably because we expect aesthetics to play some part in a design. Here on Earth we have become used to considering designs as redundancy free – there are no odds and ends left over that serve no purpose. So we are understandably unhappy with the idea that designs should contain ornaments or decorations without meaning. In other words, we want to know what purpose is served in the overall design concept by what appear to be intentionally aesthetic qualities. Having seen and appreciated a balance of tone or colour, we are keen to ascribe a further function to this aesthetic component of the design.

In imagining a design without a communicative effect, in as much as we fail to comprehend or understand the particular language being used, we more clearly see the design as open to aesthetic criticism. It has become an aesthetic object – rather as works of art are aesthetic objects. In fact, the removal of function as a means of magically transforming the ordinary into art is a trick worked by a number of artists. Classically, there are the Dada objects of Duchamp, such as his bicycle wheel, bottle rack and urinal. By denying function and rendering them unfit to perform their intended purposes, Duchamp asked us to consider such homely objects as having an alternative existence as objects of art. Of course, there is a difference between Duchamp's found objects and examples of design as design objects. For instance, we are not surprised when the aesthetic qualities of a design are pointed out, as we more or less expect designs to have these qualities in the first place.

It is possible that quite a few people, perhaps some designers, would want to deny that design can be seen under two aspects as if it was composed of two parts: an aesthetic component and a functional, communicative component. For example, some would no doubt be eager to claim that design has no business looking pretty, as it should concern itself with function alone. This kind of belief is detectable throughout the history of twentieth-century graphic design. The urge to purify designs of aesthetics accompanies a fairly widespread belief that communication ought to be a scientific affair. In this, designers are to be grouped with those who sought the underlying logic of language, who dreamt of a calculus of communication. In as much as contrary evidence never diverted a visionary or dreamer, this vein of enquiry within design has never really left us. Still, we can imagine that (somewhere), there can be found designers who are, to all intents and purposes, ignorant of aesthetics. Or, we can imagine that there are designers who believe that they have exorcized the aesthetic ghost from their work by the rigorous application of a scientific method.

One thing that the Duchamp experiments clearly show is that we can switch on our aesthetic way of seeing no matter what it is that we are looking at. When we choose to look aesthetically, we inevitably discover aesthetic qualities. Once design emerged as aesthetically self-conscious, it became impossible to reverse the process. The aura of aesthetics, of taste and style, now invariably surrounds each piece of design. It is easy to see how some designers could find this annoying. A designer with an intention to produce a simple functional design is going to be defeated in that aim, no matter how honest their effort, simply because that will not be how it is publicly received or read, unless it can be sold under some other label. Information design suggests itself as a possible suitable candidate here.

The separation of design into two components is tiresome and unsatisfactory. It does not square with our feelings or intuitions to think of aesthetics as decorative wrapping, hence as soon as we prise aesthetic qualities away from the functioning core of a design, we feel uncomfortable and want to reinstate a purpose to the aesthetic, to glue the two halves back together. Intuitively we feel that a design should be considered as a whole. If the primary aim of design is communication, then the aesthetic should somehow further that aim and not work against it. According to this view, the design as a whole is the communicating object, language and aesthetic work together in some way. This holistic concept of design is persuasive but it is not immediately clear how it works in practice.

Suppose a design, at first glance, puts us in a particular mood, due to its formal configurations. Just a glimpse of colour, for example, can induce such a mood.[1] This mood could be happy or sad in character. Or, it may be a mood of a more undecided kind, perhaps a relaxed or daydreaming and speculative frame of mind. Whatever the particularities of effect – and there would seem to be an almost endless list of possibilities – it may be that the induced mood is somehow conducive to some special interpretation of the design. So, when we get round to registering any linguistic message we tend to favour one set of interpretations over others.[2] A preference is set up that allows for an economy of means in so far as the quantity of words in the design is concerned. In fact, there may be many ways in which such a bias or frame of mind could ease the problem of understanding.

With our imaginary alien example, we did not understand the language used but nevertheless a context of understanding was set up. Images and thoughts inspired by a design which we look at but have not read flood our minds and prime us for the more explicit communication of language.

When communicating, it is more than useful to have some idea of the state of mind of your audience. What beliefs, preconceptions and predilections does your audience have? Our words may be misunderstood, meanings can go astray. Mistakes of meaning can be avoided only if we put in some work on preparing our audience for what is to be said. Aesthetics is one such means of preparation at the disposal of designers.

It may be objected that things could proceed in the reverse order – we read first and then become aware of the look of the design – but this would not essentially alter the mechanics of communication. Reading first simply puts meaning on hold until such time as the relevant aesthetic context is supplied. Whichever order of events corresponds to any particular experience of a design, it is evident that communication is achieved over a span of time. The exact duration may well vary from design to design and from audience to audience. In the imaginary alien example, understanding may be a long time coming and we would certainly have abandoned any mood or frame of mind induced by the design long before. There would appear to be limits as to how much we can stretch a design over time because there are limits to an audience's tolerances.

Practical considerations dictate that a design be taken in at a glance, or certainly in a short period of time. Graphic designers are not alone in wishing to communicate quickly and efficiently. Some theories of communication and language support the idea of codes of behaviour in communicative exchanges. In other words, we learn what to expect of others when they attempt to communicate. Some such codes or rules of communicative behaviour do appear to include injunctions to keep our communications simple and to the point.[3] When a designer indulges the aesthetic it would seem that some of those codes of communicative behaviour are broken. Yet this need not invariably be disastrous to any communicative intention. We may still be able to work out what the meaning is.

On the whole, however, unexpected behaviour takes up more time and effort on the part of an audience. If a design is too aesthetically absorbing then understanding could be delayed.

So far, the assumption has been that design is about getting across a single message. True enough, many designs are unquestionably of this kind, but equally, many others are not. We can therefore expect there to be a value in designs without specific meanings.

Tracing back the process of design production to that strange relationship between designer, brief and client, we could point to this as the origin of a design's communicative intentions. Messages, definite or not, develop, or even grow, out of this relationship. In so far as design communication resembles ordinary communication, it is reasonable to expect simple, definite messages. As we have seen, most of our daily discourse is based upon this assumption that there are end points to the communicative exchanges that we share with each other. Those end points are determinate meanings. Without this we would hardly get much done. And, on the whole, this all works pretty well; most of the time communication is effective and our actions are informed. Even children get the hang of it. Yet the purposes of language and communication in general often mirrors this variety. Getting across one meaning, being straightforwardly informative, is only one of a number of possible communicative intentions.[4]

This is not the place to explore the numerous purposes and aims of communication or design, but one thing seems clear: the further we move away from the central informative intention the more likely it is that aesthetics will figure prominently. The reason for this is simply that language is an extremely accurate tool of communication. A thoughtful selection of words works in most circumstances. Familiarity with common situations and common phrases helps enormously to facilitate easy communication. A difference, whether new or uncommon, on the other hand, can cause problems.

Vagueness of meaning is again something we associate with art; perhaps with literary as well as visual forms. With a work of art we are used to the idea that meaning is somehow up for grabs. Meaning in the arts is something that is argued about by critics. Such argued meaning may never be ultimately fixed. A critic can always justify their reading of a new meaning. The question for design is whether or not this kind of vagueness of meaning is useful.

With works of art, the meanings constructed by critics are evidence of a psychological relationship between critic and work of art. Some might see this relationship as possessive in character; that the critic encompasses the artwork with their thoughts and justifications. In one sense this may be the nearest we can get to actually owning works of art.

In a similar fashion the vagueness of design could invite us to speculate and create our own meanings. This is akin to how we customize our possessions, taking mass produced products – cars, houses, clothes and so on – and adjusting them to conform to our designs and fantasies. Just as we customize products, so we customize meanings.

Advertising graphics demonstrates how this could work. In advertising, aesthetic features such as forms, colours and images are accentuated above words. Often only the name of a product is found in an advertisement, the rest consists of a powerful display of aesthetics; images, forms and colours combine to suggest routes through to meaning.[5] The hope of advertisers is to get their product mixed up with our created meanings. As the meanings are ours, so the product becomes ours – we own it before we have even spent any money.

Design may attempt to minimize aesthetic responses in an audience but it cannot dispense with aesthetics entirely because we can all turn on our aesthetic vision whenever we wish. Usually we do this only when invited to by an appropriate stimulus.[6] In the past, perhaps, appropriate stimuli were works of art. Now we must also include design.

References

Introduction
Teal Triggs

1   Frascara, Jorge, 'Graphic Design; Audience at the Center', *Design Statements*, Winter 1993, p. 10.

Redefining Men: *Arena* Magazine, Image and Identity
David Cook

1   Hunt, R., 'The schlock of the new new', in Media *Guardian*, 28 January 1991.

2   Dylan Jones, in conversation with the author, 20 April 1993.

3   ibid.

4   ibid.

5   ibid.

6   Owen, William, *Magazine Design*, Lawrence King, 1991, p. 116.

7   Rutherford, Jonathan, 'Who's That Man', in *Male Order: Unwrapping Masculinity*, Lawrence and Wishart, 1988, p. 38.

8   'Fin de Siècle', *Arena*, Wagadon, issue 7, Winter 1987–8.

9   op.cit., Jones.

Our Image of the Third World
Geoff Warren

1   Galbraith, John K., *The Nature of Mass Poverty*, Penguin Books, 1980, p. 20.

2   Clarke, John, *For Richer for Poorer*, Oxfam, 1986, p. 15.

References

Venereal Disease Propaganda in the Second World War
Joanna Close

1   See Hebdige, Dick, 'Object as Image: the Italian Scooter Cycle' in *Hiding in the Light: On Images and Things*, Comedia, 1988.

2   Judith Williamson has written that 'my interest has never been so much in adverts, as in what they show about our society and ways of seeing ourselves'. (Williamson, *Decoding Advertisements: Ideology and Meaning in Advertising*, Marion Boyars, 1978, Preface to the Fourth Edition).

3   See Bourdieu, Pierre, *Distinction: A Social Critique of the Judgement of Taste*, Routledge and Kegan Paul, 1984, p. 126. In discussing sociological discourse, Bourdieu points out that 'One of the difficulties...lies in the fact that like all discourse, it unfolds in strictly linear fashion whereas, to escape over-simplification and one-sidedness one needs to be able to recall at every point the whole network of relationships found there'.

4   The Mass-Observation Archive is at the University of Sussex Library. Dorothy Sheridan, Archivist, explains that, 'Founded in 1937 by a group of young, upper-class male intellectuals it set out to create what it called "an anthropology of ourselves". It challenged the claim of the press to represent ordinary people and, by its unique blend of anthropology, American-influenced sociology and psychoanalysis, endeavoured to tap a deeper level of human consciousness in the British social character...The central tenet of their approach was to "observe": to watch and to record people's behaviour and conversations.' (Sheridan, ed., *Wartime Women: An Anthology of Women's Wartime Writing for Mass-Observation 1937–45,* Heinemann, 1990, p. 4).

5   By mid 1941, British VD statistics showed an increase of 70 per cent compared to those at the outbreak of war and 'in London and the seaports the rise was more dramatic, with Liverpool's health authorities reporting an alarming four-fold increase in syphilis cases, with the rate "still rising"' (see Costello, John, *Love, Sex and War: Changing Values 1939–45,* Pan Books, 1986, p. 127.) By 1943, the incidence of VD was 139 per cent higher than at the commencement of war (see Minns, Raynes, *Bombers and Mash: The Domestic Front 1939–1945*, Virago, 1980, p. 179).

6   For example, Costello states (p. 127) 'The arrival of the first American troops on British soil in the spring of 1942 sent venereal disease to almost epidemic proportions'.

7   Quoted by Costello, p. 328.

8   *Mass-Observation Report* 1633, 20 March 1943, p. 3. The Report's

'Introductory' (p. 1) describes the survey as 'A small check study…to probe people's feelings about and attitudes to Government V.D. publicity'. 24 per cent of those questioned disapproved of the press advertisements – either on moral grounds and/or because of embarrassment, or because they felt the advertising to be in some way deficient, e.g. 'I feel they're [the advertisements] not explicit enough or nearly helpful enough.'

9   *Mass-Observation Report* 1573, 4 January 1943, p. 19. This survey of people's attitudes to and opinions about VD was conducted in three London boroughs: Poplar, Fulham and Balham and Tooting. 435 direct interviews were obtained and the survey sample was predominantly working class. Slightly more men than women were interviewed.

10   Mass-Observation surveys show that Regulation 33B was welcomed by the majority of British people (see for example, *Mass-Observation Report* 1573).

11   See Morton, R. S., *Sexual Freedom and Venereal Disease*, Peter Owen, 1971, pp. 105–6.

12   The Imperial War Museum, London holds a number of examples of British and American Second World War posters concerned with venereal disease. The Museum also houses a collection of photographs and a public information film on the subject.

13   Reginald Mount, a designer employed by Britain's Ministry of Information during the war, draws a distinction between 'easy girl-friend' and 'prostitute' when discussing the concept behind one of his venereal disease posters (see Darracott, Joseph and Loftus, Belinda, *Second World War Posters*, Imperial War Museum, 1981, p. 47). I suggest that prostitution is none the less implicit in the message conveyed by Mount's amalgamation of copy and imagery.

14   I met Dr J. M. Dunlop, the former Medical Officer of Health for Hull (and an army doctor during the war) on a train in 1988. I was reading a book about venereal disease and he was en route to a major AIDS conference. Not surprisingly, our conversation centred on sexually transmitted disease. He recollected American matchboxes warning against VD in circulation during the war.

15   A 1944 US Army 'Warning to all ranks' (Imperial War Museum) declares that Italy 'has always been…a hotbed of Venereal Disease' and that an infected woman 'can look youthful, clean, attractive…So don't be hoodwinked'. The Americans set up VD treatment centres, dubbed 'Casanova Camps'. Thesewere reportedly surrounded by barbed wire – to keep infected men in and the Italian women (infected but untreated) out. (See Costello, pp. 305–6.)

16 I conducted a taped interview with F. H. K. Henrion at his home in London in April 1988.

17 Quoted by Costello, p. 81.

18 See *The Times*, 28 October 1943, p. 8.

19 Wilson Jameson, Chief Medical Officer, Ministry of Health, quoted by Costello, p. 329.

20 I talked with Abram Games at his home in London in the autumn of 1988.

21 'Clean living is the real safeguard' was a core slogan in the 'Let Knowledge Grow' campaign.

Generation Terrorists: Fanzines and Communication
Teal Triggs

1 Gunderloy, Mike and Janice, Cari Goldberg, *The World of Zines: A Guide to the Independent Magazine Revolution*, Penguin Books, 1992, p. 2.

2 Fanzines are distributed through the post with readers supplying a SASE with a nominal amount of money covering the basic production and postage costs. See 'Fanzine Report', by Piglet, *The Zine*, Issue 5, December/January 93/4, p. 70.

3 This article in *The Zine* offered advice to readers for first time publishing ventures. See Jasper Bark, 'Off the Page and Into Print', *The Zine*, Issue 5, December/January 93/4, p. 64.

4 Janice, Cari Goldberg, introduction to Trusky, Tom, *Some Zines: American Alternative and Underground Magazines, Newsletters and APAs*, Boise State University, 1992, p. ii.

5 Occasionally the fanzine has been referred to as an 'amazine', highlighting the amateur nature of its editorial and print production. See *Oxford English Dictionary*, Volume V (2nd edition), p. 810.

6 Nicholls, Peter, *The Encyclopedia of Science Fiction: An Illustrated A to Z*, Granta, 1979, p. 237.

7 Wyness, Andy, editor, *Peter Weller is Back*, Issue 1, October 1991, n.p.

8 Editor of *UK Resist* writing in Rutherford, Paul, ed., *Fanzine Culture*, Clydeside Press, 1992, p. 16.

9   *The Zine*, Issue 1, July 1993, p. 1.

10 Clarke, John, Hall, Stuart, Jefferson, Tony and Roberts, Brian, 'Subcultures, Cultures and Class' in Hall, Stuart and Jefferson, Tony, eds., *Resistance Through Rituals: Youth Subcultures in Post-War Britain*, Hutchinson, 1986, p. 13.

11 Williams, Raymond, *Communications*, Penguin Books, 1989, p. 50–51.

12 Jon Savage credits Brian Hogg with producing the first fanzine in Britain, *Bam Balam*, focusing on the late 1960s music scene. See Savage, Jon, *England's Dreaming*, Faber and Faber, 1991, p. 201.

13 Widgery, David, 'Underground Press', in *International Socialism*, no. 51, April/June, 1972, p. 3.

14 Henry, Tricia, *Break All Rules! Punk Rock and the Making of a Style*, UMI Research Press, 1989, p. 96. Most recently, *Birth of a Hooligan* (c. 1992), a fanzine directed at 'politically correct' skinheads, has published on the back page of Issue 2 'Rights on Arrest Advice', which states procedures and an individual's legal rights if stopped by the police.

15 Home, Stewart, *The Assault on Culture: Utopian Current From Lettrisme to Class War*, AK Press, 1991, p. 84.

16 Frith, Simon, *Sound Effects: Youth, Leisure and the Politics of Rock*, Constable, 1983, p. 177.

17 ibid., p. 175.

18 'A Victim of Innocence', *Off the Wall*, Issue 23, Winter, 1993/4, p. 13.

19 The editor, *What's This Generation Coming To?* Issue 2, 1983, n.p.

Solidarity: Subversive Codes for Social Change
Diane J. Gromala

1   Kovacs, Tom, 'The Spirit of Metaphor: An Alternative Visual Language', *Icographic*, 1983:4.

2   Boczar, Danuta A., 'The Polish Poster', *Art Journal*, Spring 1994, p. 19–20.

3   Frascara, Jorge, 'Graphic Design, Possibilities, Responsibilities?', *Projekt*, February 1990, pp. 35–6.

4   Crimp, Douglas with Rolston, Adam, *AIDS: Demographics*, Bay Press, 1990.

5   In this sense, ideology not as false consciousness but as those values and interests that inform any representation of reality. See Mitchell, W. J. T., *Iconography: Image, Text, Ideology*, The University of Chicago Press, 1987.

6   Palaszewska, Miroslawa, Director of the Muzeum Historii Polskich Ruchow Niepodleglosciowych i Spolezuych (Museum of Polish Independence Movements), personal interview, 24 July 1991, Warsaw.
Artists, designers and other creators of work for Solidarity sometimes came forward to claim authorship after elections in 1989, when several Polish museums began collections of Solidarity artefacts. Some of this material came directly from former secret police confiscations.

7   Konstrukcja w Procesie (Construction in Process), Lodz, Poland. See documents based on this large exhibition of international contemporary art. It was organized outside of official state channels, 'an event without precedent in post-war Poland' which coincided with the founding of the a.r. (revolutionary artists) group of constructivists.

8   Weschler, Lawrence, 'Solidarity', *Art Forum*, February 1982, pp. 36–42.

9   The Solidarity logo was designed in Gdansk in August of 1980 during the Lenin Shipyard strikes by brothers and graphic designers J. and K. Janiszewski.

10   Dr Szymon Bojko, personal interview, 30 July 1991, Warsaw.

11   Hughes, H. Stuart, *Sophisticated Rebels: The Political Culture of European Dissent, 1968–87*, Harvard University Press, 1990, p. 80.

12   ibid., p. 82.

13   ibid., p. 81.

14   Perlez, Jane, 'Job Shake-Out Pushes Poles to Ex-Communists', *The New York Times*, 18 September 1993, International, p. 4.

15   Piotr Mlodozeniec, personal interview, 27 July 1991, Warsaw.

Organizing a Counter-culture with Graffiti: The Tsoi Wall and its Antecedents
John Bushnell

1   For a history of Soviet graffiti and counter-culture through to 1989, see Bushnell, John *Moscow Graffiti: Language and Subculture*, Unwin Hyman, 1990.

118

Post-photography: The Highest Stage of Photography
Kevin Robins

1 Cotton, Bob and Oliver, Richard, eds., *Understanding Hypermedia: From Multimedia to Virtual Reality*, Phaidon Press, 1993.

2 Robins, Kevin, 'Into the Image' in Wombell, Paul, ed., *Photovideo: Photography in the Age of the Computer*, Rivers Oram Press, 1991; Robins, Kevin, 'The Virtual Unconscious in Post-Photography', *Science as Culture*, no. 14, 1992.

3 Höch, Hannah, 'A Few Words on Photomontage', in Lavin, Maud, ed., *Cut With the Kitchen Knife: The Weimar Photomontages of Hannah Höch*, Yale University Press, 1993, p. 219.

4 ibid., p. 220.

5 Sontag, Susan, *On Photography*, Penguin, 1979, p. 123.

6 Lawson, Jim, 'Calum Colvin and Deadly Sins', *Portfolio*, no. 17, Summer 1993, p. 7.

7 David Bailey quoted in Rocque, Melony, 'Camera Obscura', *XYZ*, September 1993, p. 23.

8 See Ritchin, Fred, '*In Our Own Image: The Coming Revolution in Photography*', Aperture, 1990; Becker, Karen E., 'To Control Our Image: Photojournalists and New Technology', *Media Culture and Society*, vol. 13, no. 3, 1991.

9 Mitchell, William, J., *The Reconfigured Eye: Visual Truth in the Post-Photographic Era*, MIT Press, 1992, p. 8.

Turning on to Television
Michèle-Anne Dauppe

1 See for example, Laughton, Roy, *TV Graphics*, 1966; Merrit, Douglas, *Television Graphics – From Pencil to Pixel*, 1987; Crook, Geoffrey, *The Changing Image: Television Graphics from Caption Card to Computer*, 1986.

2 See the essays by Buscombe, Ed and Hartley, John in ed., Masterman, Len, *Television Mythologies*, 1984; Morey, John, *The Space between Programmes: Television Continuity*, University of London Institute of Education, 1981. The BFI teaching pack entitled 'Starters' analyses title sequences and titling is given some consideration in, for example, Masterman, Len, *Teaching Television*, 1980. The chapter 'Programming: distribution and flow' in Raymond Williams's seminal book *Television, Technology and Cultural Form* is also useful.

References

3   Research was limited to BBC1, BBC2, ITV and Channel 4.

4   As a guide, within a typical weekday's broadcast, junctions between pro-
    grammes on BBC1 amount to 28 minutes and on BBC2 to 37 minutes. This is
    equivalent to 2.3 per cent and 3.5 per cent of output respectively (figures
    obtained from junction schedule for Tuesday, October 12, 1993, supplied by
    the BBC).

5   Channel 4, Saturday 16 October 1993 – television graphics preceding 'Rory
    Bremner – Who Else?', 10.05.

6   'Poems on the Box' was broadcast on BBC2 during the week beginning
    11 October 1993.

7   Williams, Raymond *Television, Technology and Cultural Form*, 1990.

8   ibid., p. 86.

9   ibid., pp. 90–1.

10 Ellis, John, *Visible Fictions*, 1992, p. 117.

11 op. cit., Morey, John, p. 117.

12 For a discussion of the implications of the digital image and photography see
    Rosler, Martha, 'Image Simulations Computer Manipulations: some considera-
    tions' in Ten-8, *Digital Dialogues*, vol. 2, no. 2, Autumn, 1991.

13 op cit., Morey, pp. 4–5.

14 op. cit., Buscombe, p. 129.

15 op. cit., Buscombe, p. 130.

16 Both were produced by Diverse Design using a range of videographic tech-
    niques with archive and purpose shot film footage and collage effects.

Visual Rhetoric and Semiotics
Edward Triggs

1   Chaim Perelman points out that 'as soon as communication tries to influence
    one or more persons, to orient their thinking, to excite or calm emotions, to
    guide their actions, it belongs to the realm of rhetoric.' See Perelman, C., *The
    Realm of Rhetoric*, trans. William Kluback, University of Notre Dame Press,
    1982, p. 162. This can be extended to any area of printed communication in

that 'text and images are always produced by particular people with particular purposes, and so bear the traces of human intention'. Kinross, Robin, 'Semiotics and Designing', *Information Design Journal 4*, 1986, p. 192.

2   Hanno H. J. Ehses details the steps of the classical rhetorical system in 'Rhetoric and Design', *Icographic* 2, 4, March 1984, pp. 4–6, and Roland Barthes provides a comprehensive overview of the history of rhetoric in *The Semiotic Challenge*, trans. Richard Howard, Hill and Wang, 1988, pp. 11–94.

3   'Rhetorica', trans. W. Rhys Roberts, in *The Basic Works of Aristotle*, ed. Richard McKeon, Random House, 1941, p. 1329.

4   Popper, Karl, P., *Objective Knowledge: An Evolutionary Approach*, Oxford University Press, revised edition, 1979, p. 154.

5   For a comprehensive discussion of argumentation, see Perelman, *Realm of Rhetoric*, pp. 21–32, 53–113.

6   'Metaphysics', trans. W. D. Ross, *The Basic Works of Aristotle*, ed. McKeon, Random House, 1941, p. 796.

7   Imitations of things or parts of things hold greater interest than do the objects they imitate as humans 'delight in seeing likenesses because in contemplating them it happens that they are learning and reasoning out what each thing is…' Telford, Kenneth A., *Aristotle's Poetics: Translation and Analysis*, Gateway Editions, 1961, p. 6.

8   For a comprehensive discussion of semiotics, see Eco, Umberto, *A Theory of Semiotics*, Indiana University Press, 1976.

9   ibid., pp. 48–9.

10   In the 'Verbal Graphic Language' of Michael Twyman, the graphic branch of the visual channel of language is divided into verbal, pictorial and schematic. Verbal being words; pictorial being drawings and photographs; and schematic encompassing all graphic marks which are not words or pictures. Twyman, Michael, 'The Graphic Presentation of Language', *Information Design Journal* 3, 1982, p. 7.

11   Roland Barthes generalizes Aristotle's comments on the three options a speaker has when deciding the tone of a presentation: projecting the quality of one who deliberates, showing frankness, or being sympathetic. Barthes, *The Semiotic Challenge*, trans., Richard Howard, Hill and Wang, 1988, p. 74. The intention is to keep utterances of aesthetic value, style or designer 'artistry' to a minimum so as to establish a tone of frankness for the message.

References

12 After the completion of this piece, I came across a similar analysis presented by John A. Walker of Klaus Staeck's Poster and Postcard, 1971, a montage of a pet food advertisement superimposed upon an image of a starving child. For further discussion see Walker, John A., *Art in the Age of Mass Media*, Pluto Press, 1983, p. 98.

13 A rectangular shape of text (having proportions similar to the shape of the photo) placed in the centre of the screened photo (as in the previous example of starving children) reinforces the plane of the page which effectively 'pushes' the photo back into space. This juxtaposition of the text also suggests a denial of the photo and a negation of the children, both notions reinforcing the idea of 'vanishing'.

14 In classical rhetoric, figures are used to embellish major parts of an argument so as to increase persuasiveness. Gui Bonsepe presents a catalogue of rhetorical figures and their use in analysing the persuasiveness of advertisements in 'Visual/Verbal Rhetoric', *Dot Zero 2*, 1966, pp. 37–42.

15 Perelman, *Realm of Rhetoric*, p. 38.

The London Underground Diagram
John A. Walker

1 Garland, Ken, 'The Design of the London Underground Diagram', *Penrose Annual*, vol. 62, ed. H. Spencer, Lund Humphries, 1969, pp. 68–82. See also, Garland, 'Obituary: Henry C. Beck', *Design*, (312), December 1974, p. 86. There are two further short articles: Berger, Arthur, 'London's Underground as a work of art', *San Francisco Chronicle*, 12 June 1975, p. 21; Penrice, Leonard, 'The London Underground Diagram', *Graphic Lines* (1), 1975, pp. 19–22.

2 Typewritten statement by Beck in possession of Ken Garland.

3 Morris, Charles, *Signs, language and behaviour*, Braziller, 1955, p. 23.

4 Penrice, 'The London Underground Diagram'.

5 Pierce quoted in Greenlee, D., *Pierce's Concept of Signs*, Mouton, 1973, p. 55.

6 Barthes, Roland, *Rhetoric of the Image, Working papers in Cultural Studies (1)*, Spring 1971.

Design, Communication and the Functioning Aesthetic
David Rowsell

1   See Mulvey, J., 'Pictures with words: a critique of Alain-Marie Bassy's approach', *Information Design Journal*, vol. 5/2, 197, pp. 141–158. Mulvey makes a comparison between pictures with words and the stage, where scenery allows us to interpret the actions of actors.

2   This kind of analysis of language, with its emphasis on the contexts of inter-pretation is known as 'pragmatics'. A fairly accessible discussion of contempo-rary developments in pragmatics is given in Sperber, D. and Wilson, D., *Relevance*, Blackwell, 1986.

3   Grice has outlined a number of 'maxims' which seem to govern ordinary con-versation. Grice, H. P., 'Logic and Conversation', in Cole, P. and Morgan, J., *Syntax and Semantics 9: Pragmatics*, New York, 1978.

4   Austin, J. L., *How to do things with words*, Clarendon Press, 1962.

5   Similar approaches to the understanding of advertisements can be found in Pateman, T., 'How is understanding an advertisement possible? in eds., Davis and Walton, *Language, Image, Media*, Blackwell, 1983, pp. 187–204. See also, Davidson, M., *The Consumerist Manifesto*, Routledge, 1992, pp. 143–163.

6   This is of course the role of design in taste formation and the evolution of styles. This is a cultural view of aesthetic value rather than the less satisfying formalist alternative – where one is restricted to the 'visual semantics' of an aesthetic object. For a useful discussion of taste, see, Lloyd Jones, Peter, *Taste Today*, Oxford, 1991.

Further Reading

124

Ashwin, Clive, *History of Graphic Design and Communication: A Sourcebook*, 1983

Barthes, Roland, *Camera Lucida*, translated Richard Howard, Fontana Paperbacks, 1984 reprint

Barthes, Roland, *Image/Music/Text*, translated Stephen Heath, Hill and Wang, 1977

Barthes, Roland, *Mythologies*, translated Annette Lavers, Paladin Grafton Books, 1987 reprint

Benjamin, Walter, *Illuminations*, Schoken Books, 1978

Berger, John, *Ways of Seeing*, Penguin, 1972

Blonsky, Marshall, ed., *On Signs*, John Hopkins University Press, 1985

Bolton, Richard, ed., *The Contest of Meaning: Critical Histories of Photography*, The MIT Press, 1989

Culler, Jonathan, *On Deconstruction: Theory and Criticism after Structuralism*, Cornell University Press, 1989

Derrida, Jacques, *Of Grammatology*, John Hopkins University Press, 1976

Eco, Umberto, *Travels in Hyperreality*, Harcourt, Brace, Jovanovich, 1986

Ewen, Stuart, *All Consuming Images: The Politics of Style in Contemporary Culture*, Basic Books, 1988

Forty, Adrian, *Objects of Desire: Design and Society Since 1750*, Thames and Hudson, 1986

Glauber, Barbara, ed., *Lift and Separate: Graphic Design and the Vernacular*, The Cooper Union for the Advancement of Science and Art, 1993

Hawkes, Terrence, *Structuralism and Semiotics*, Methuen, 1986 reprint

Hebdige, Dick, *Hiding in the Light: On Images and Things*, Routledge, 1988

Jenkins, Janet, *In the Spirit of Fluxus*, Walker Art Center, 1993

Latimer, Dan, *Contemporary Critical Theory*, Harcourt, Brace, Jovanovich, 1989

Lovejoy, Margot, *Postmodern Currents: Art and Artists in the Age of Electronic Media*, Prentice Hall, 1992

Margolin, Victor, ed., *Design Discourse: History, Theory, Criticism* University of Chicago Press, 1989

McLuhan, Marshall, *The Gutenberg Galaxy: The Making of Typographic Man*, University of Toronto Press, 1962

McLuhan, Marshall and Fior, Quentin, *The Medium is the Massage*, Bantam Books, 1967

McLuhan, Marshall, *Understanding Media: The Extensions of Man*, McGraw-Hill Book Company, 1964

McLuhan, Marshall and Powers, Bruce R., *The Global Village: Transformations in World Life and Media in the 21st Century*, Oxford University Press, 1989

McQuiston, Liz, *Graphic Agitation: Social and Political Graphics Since the Sixties*, Phaidon, 1993

McQuiston, Liz, *Women in Design: A Contemporary View*, Rizzoli, 1988

Ong, Walter, *Orality and Literacy: The Technologizing of the Word*, Methuen, 1992

Postman, Neil, *Amusing Ourselves to Death*, Methuen, 1987

Ronell, Avital, *The Telephone Book: Technology, Schizophrenia, Electric Speech*, University of Nebraska Press, 1989

Roszak, Theodore, *The Cult of Information: The Folklore of Computers and the True Art of Thinking*, Lutterworth Press, 1986

Smith, Virginia, *The Funny Little Man: the Biography of a Graphic Image*, Van Nostrand Reinhold, 1993

Squires, Carol, *The Critical Image: Essays on Contemporary Photography*, Lawrence and Wishart, 1990

Sussman, Elizabeth, ed., *On the Passage of a Few People Through a Rather Brief Moment in Time: The Situationist International 1957–1972*, The MIT Press, 1989

Taylor, Mark C. and Saarinen, Esa, *Imagologies: Media Philosophy*, Routledge, 1994

Tufte, Edward R., *Envisioning Information*, Graphics Press, 1990

Walker, John A., *Art in the Age of Mass Media*, Pluto Press, 1983

Williams, Raymond, *Communications*, Penguin Books, 1962

Williamson, Judith, *Decoding Advertisements: Ideology and Meaning in Advertising*, Marion Boyars, 1978

Index

Index

DISCOVER THROUGH CRAFT

RAINFORESTS

By Jillian Powell

W

Franklin Watts
Published in Great Britain in 2017
by The Watts Publishing Group

Series editor: Amy Stephenson
Series designer: Jeni Child
Crafts: Rita Storey
Craft photography: Tudor Photography
Picture researcher: Diana Morris

Dewey number: 333.7'5
ISBN: 978 1 4451 5490 9

Printed in China

Franklin Watts
An imprint of Hachette Children's Group
Part of The Watts Publishing Group
Carmelite House
50 Victoria Embankment
London EC4Y 0DZ

An Hachette UK Company
www.hachette.co.uk
www.franklinwatts.co.uk

FSC
MIX
Paper from
responsible sources
FSC® C104740

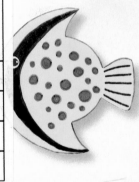

CONTENTS

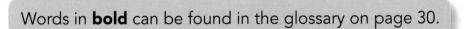

Words in **bold** can be found in the glossary on page 30.

Some of the projects in this book require scissors, paint and glue. We would recommend that children are supervised by a responsible adult when using these things.

ABOUT RAINFORESTS

Every rainforest is different but they are all alike in some key ways.

Moist air hangs above the rainforest canopy.

What are rainforests?

Rainforests are forests of tall trees. They grow in warm or cool **climates** that have lots of rain all year round. Rainforest trees grow close together to form a **canopy** of leaves and branches that grow high above the ground. The tallest trees can reach heights of 60 metres. Rainforests are home to many kinds of plants and animals.

QUIZ TIME!

Which rainforest is the largest in the world?

a. the Amazon

b. the Congo

c. Daintree

Answer on page 32.

Where are they found?

There are two main kinds of rainforest. Tropical rainforests grow in the **tropics**, between the Tropic of Cancer and the Tropic of Capricorn, either side of the Earth's **Equator**. Here it stays warm and wet all year round. Some rainforests have more than 2.5 centimetres of rain nearly every day of the year. There are tropical rainforests in parts of Africa, Asia, Australia and Central and South America. **Temperate** rainforests grow along coasts in temperate zones, which lie between the tropics and the polar circles. The climate is cooler here but still mild and the air is often damp with mist, fog and rain. There are temperate rainforests in North America, Norway, Japan, New Zealand, South Australia, Ireland and the United Kingdom.

KEY:

Countries with the largest area of tropical rainforest:
1 Brazil
2 Democratic Republic of Congo
3 Peru
4 Indonesia
5 Colombia.

Largest area of temperate rainforest:
6 The Pacific coast, North America.

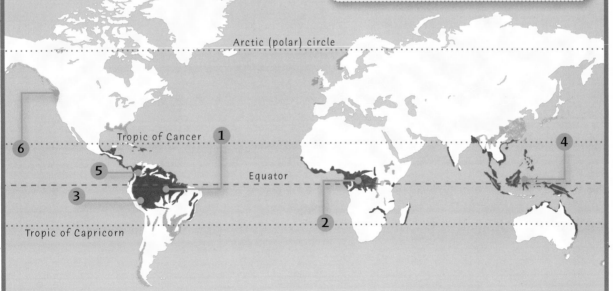

Arctic (polar) circle

Tropic of Cancer

Equator

Tropic of Capricorn

Quick FACTS

• Rainforests are forests with tall trees growing in either warm or cool climates.
• They have lots of rain all year round.
• They are home to many kinds of plants and animals.

WHY ARE RAINFORESTS IMPORTANT?

Rainforests are important because they protect the people and animals that live in them – and the whole planet.

Bengal tigers live in tropical rainforests in Asia.

A rich habitat

Rainforests provide a home for millions of plants and animals, including **mammals**, insects, birds and fish. Although they only cover about 6% of the Earth's surface, they contain half of all the plant and animal **species** on Earth. They are also home to **tribal** peoples who rely on the forest for shelter and food. Many of the medicines we use come from rainforest plants.

Climate

The trees and plants in rainforests soak up water through their roots, then release it as moisture through their leaves. The moisture helps to form rain clouds, which produce rainfall, both in the forest and around the world. Rainforests have also been called 'the lungs of the world' because they take in **carbon dioxide** from the **atmosphere** and produce **oxygen**, which all living things need to live and grow. Too much carbon dioxide can warm the Earth's atmosphere and cause **climate change** (p. 27) so rainforests help to keep our climate stable.

Soil and erosion

Tree roots help to keep soil in place, but when trees are cut down, the soil can wash away. This is called erosion. The roots of rainforest trees help stop rainwater flooding the land and stop soil from being washed away into rivers, where it can harm fish and other wildlife. The trees also help to keep soil and rocks in place on hillsides, where erosion can cause landslides. Landslides can be dangerous and threaten people, animals and their homes.

Quick FACTS

Rainforests:
- Produce rainfall around the world.
- Help keep the climate stable.
- Provide a home for people, plants and animals.
- Provide food and medicines.
- Help stop erosion and flooding.

? Why do you think the rainforest is such a rich **habitat** for plants and animals? Turn the page to find out.

The rainforest has three main habitats that are rich in animal and plant life.

Overstory

Canopy

Understory

Forest floor

The canopy

As rainforest trees grow tall their branches get squashed together. This forms a thick canopy where other plants grow and animals find food and shelter. Most rainforest animals and plants live up in the canopy – some will never touch the forest floor! Giant trees that grow even taller than the canopy form a top layer or 'overstory'.

HAVE A GO
Collect vegetable peelings and put them in a compost bin at home or at school. The peelings will slowly break down into a crumbly compost, which contains **nutrients** to feed growing plants.

The forest floor

The forest floor is under the cover of the canopy so it stays moist and shady. **Fungi**, mosses, insects and tiny living things called **microbes** (p. 11) live here. They help to **recycle** dead leaves and other animal and plant matter by breaking them down. Between the forest floor and the canopy is a layer called the 'understory' where smaller shrubs and plants grow.

Rivers and streams

The high rainfall feeds rivers, streams and creeks. Rainforests have some of the largest rivers in the world, like the River Amazon and the Congo River. They provide a home for fish, frogs and other animals and people use the rivers to move about by boat.

Make this

Rainforests are amazing habitats that create their own climate. Make your own mini rainforest in a bottle (or terrarium) to show how water is recycled by the rainforest plants.

Put your rainforest terrarium in a spot where it will get some light and shade. Look out for condensation on the sides of the bottle. This tells you that the water is being recycled. See how long your terrarium survives.

1 Ask an adult to cut the bottom 10 cm from a 2 litre plastic bottle. Fill it half full with stones.

2 Fill the bottom with soil, but leave a 2 cm gap at the top.

3 Plant two or three small tropical houseplants (evergreens with shiny leaves). Cover the top of the soil with moss.

4 Water the plants well, then add a plastic rainforest animal. Carefully place the top half of the bottle over the plants and the bottom part. Make sure the lid is secured on tightly with tape.

RAINFOREST TREES AND PLANTS

More than half of the world's plant species are found in rainforests.

An aerial view of part of the dense canopy of the Amazon rainforest.

Canopy trees

Most tropical rainforest trees tend to grow tall and straight. There are thousands of different types. There is so much competition for water and sunlight that only one seed in 10 million grows into a tree that will reach the canopy! Many tropical trees have broad, glossy leaves that rain drips off easily.

Temperate forests can have **deciduous** trees that lose their leaves, as well as **evergreens**, such as conifers, which have needles instead of leaves. Temperate and tropical forests provide us with many things we use, such as wood, fruit, rubber, medicines, chocolate and spices.

HAVE A GO
Try growing a tropical plant using mango, papaya or avocado seeds, after you've eaten the fruit. You can try sprouting seeds in water or plant them straight into moist compost.

Tree trunks act as supports for vines and other plants.

Liana vines

Lianas are a type of climbing vine that have thick woody stems. They use roots or **tendrils** to attach themselves to trees and climb by winding themselves around the trunk or branches. When they reach the top of a tree, they can spread to other trees or wind around other lianas to form super-strong vines. Some can grow up to 900 metres long.

Smaller trees and plants

Palm trees, young saplings and shrubs grow in the understory, under the shade of the canopy. Sometimes a canopy tree comes crashing down. This lets in more light, which encourages more plants to grow.

Fungi and microbes

On the forest floor, where it is warm, damp and shady, fungi and tiny living things called microbes grow. They help break down dead plant or animal matter into nutrients. This process is called decomposition. Trees and plants take these nutrients up through their roots as food.

Many kinds of fungi grow on dead and rotting wood in the rainforest.

? **What other kinds of plants grow in the rainforest? Turn the page to find out.**

One tree can support lots of different types of epiphytes, such as these bromeliads.

Epiphytes

Epiphytes or 'air plants' grow on the branches and trunks of other trees and plants. They grow from seeds or **spores** carried by birds, animals or the wind. Mosses and ferns grow in temperate rainforests. Orchids, **bromeliads** and cacti grow in tropical rainforests. Some epiphytes, like the strangler fig, send long roots down to the ground to find nutrients. Strangler figs can become so big they take all the nutrients from the tree they are growing on and kill it!

Carnivorous plants

Some plants in the rainforest are **carnivorous**. This means they get food or nutrients from insects, spiders or even lizards and other small animals. Pitcher plants are shaped like tubes. They have a slippery surface so insects slide down into a sugary liquid inside. When the insect drowns and rots in the liquid, the plant soaks up the nutrients. Other plants have sticky hairs on their leaves to trap insects or they snap shut when an insect crawls inside.

QUIZ TIME!

How tall do you think most canopy trees grow in the rainforest?

a. **15 metres**

b. **45 metres**

c. **65 metres**

Answer on page 32.

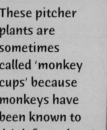

These pitcher plants are sometimes called 'monkey cups' because monkeys have been known to drink from them!

Make this

Pitcher plants love the nutrients from a juicy insect or spider. Make these pitcher plants and play a game of fly tiddlywinks to see how many will be eaten! You can play against your friends and keep score.

Now you're ready to play the game. Keep score of how many you get into each pot. One point for pot 1, two points for pot 2 and three points for pot 3. The taller the pot the harder it is!

1 Cut cardboard tubes into three sizes – small, medium and large. Trim down the front half of each tube. Cover each tube in white paper. Tape in place and trim the paper to fit. Decorate to look like a pitcher plant (see main picture).

2 Cut three shapes, like the one shown (left), from stiff white paper. The bottom edge should be about 8 cm long. Decorate them as shown. Stick a red sticker onto each shape and give each one a number (1–3).

3 Use a pencil to curl over the top of each plant. Tape each top inside a tube.

4 Draw an insect on each of the tiddlywinks. You could draw a different type of insect for each player or use a different colour.

INSECTS AND OTHER MINIBEASTS

Lots of different kinds of insects and other minibeasts live in the rainforest.

Many minibeasts

Tropical rainforests are home to many kinds of minibeasts, such as butterflies, moths, beetles, stick insects, ants, spiders and worms. Insects are the largest group of animals that live there. Just one tree can be home to over 700 different species of insects! The rainforest provides water, shelter and food and it is warm all year round so some minibeasts are able to grow and **reproduce** all year. In temperate forests, many minibeasts live inside tree bark or on the forest floor, which is covered in dead plant and animal matter for them to feed on.

Goliath beetles live on the forest floor. They feed on rainforest fruits and climb up trees to feed on sugary tree sap.

Big and small

Rainforest insects range in size from tiny mosquitoes and ants you can hardly see, to giant beetles, spiders and some stick insects that can be 30 centimetres long. Some of the largest beetles on Earth, such as Titan and Goliath beetles, live in rainforests. They have powerful jaws for biting **prey** and sharp claws that help them to climb trees. There are also many different types and sizes of butterflies and moths. The largest grow to the size of small birds, with wingspans up to 30 centimetres across.

Beautiful tree nymph butterflies live in tropical rainforests.

HAVE A GO

Many minibeasts like living in dark, shady places like the forest floor. Make an insect habitat in the garden or at your school, using bits of wood, sticks, straw and clay flowerpots. Stack them closely together leaving small cracks for insects to hide in.

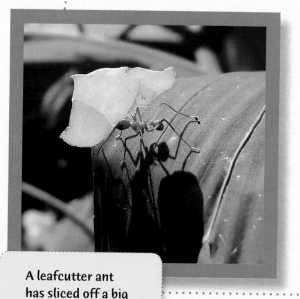

A leafcutter ant has sliced off a big piece of leaf with its powerful jaws.

Insect workers

Insects provide food for birds and other animals in the rainforest. They are also important because they help to clear the forest floor. Leafcutter ants carry leaves back to their nests. They chew up the leaves to make them into a sticky mass, which they store underground. A type of fungus grows on the chewed leaves, which the ants then eat.

? What defences do rainforest insects use to protect themselves against **predators**? Turn the page to find out.

Camouflage

Like other animals living in the rainforest, some insects use **camouflage** to hide themselves from predators. Stick insects can look like sticks or twigs. Leaf insects hang underneath trees to look like dead leaves. Some butterflies are hard to see because they look like dead leaves, or because they have wings you can see through, like the glasswing butterfly (right).

The moss mimic stick insect is camouflaged to look like the moss on a tree.

Defences

Many rainforest butterflies and moths are brightly coloured, with markings on their wings to stop predators eating them. Others have eye-like markings that make them look like animal faces. Some moth larvae look like scorpions, so predators avoid them because they think they might get stung. Caterpillars can be covered in stinging hairs or have bright patterns and colours that warn predators they may be poisonous. Bright reds, blues and yellows are common warning colours. Others use colours to look poisonous, even when they are not.

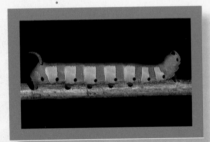

The bright colours of this caterpillar and the eye spots on the owl moth tell predators to stay away.

Quick FACTS

- Insects are the largest group of rainforest animals.
- Minibeasts can become food for birds and other animals.
- Insects also help to clear the forest floor by eating dead plants and animal matter.

Make this

Investigate the colours of rainforest butterflies. Use your research to inspire you to create this beautiful butterfly mobile.

1 Cut 10 cm circles and 10 cm squares of tissue paper. (You will need about eight of each in different colours.) Gently twist the middle of a paper circle and square. Fan out the tissue paper as shown.

2 To make one butterfly, tie a twisted circle below a twisted square with a long piece of thread. Repeat to make more butterflies.

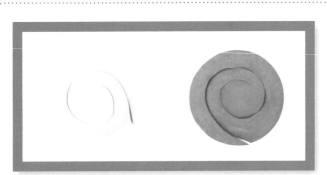

3 Draw a spiral shape on a paper plate. Cut along the line you have drawn. Paint the plate on both sides and leave to dry.

4 Tie each butterfly to your spiral to make a mobile. Hang up the mobile.

You could hang your mobile in a window so the butterflies can flutter in the breeze.

OTHER RAINFOREST ANIMALS

The rainforest is home to many different types of animal.

Who lives here?

All kinds of animals, from elephants and tigers to bats, frogs and snakes, live in tropical rainforests. Many of the larger animals live on the forest floor, but lots of smaller animals live in the canopy. They use loud calls to communicate and move around by jumping, swinging or gliding through the trees. Spider monkeys, from South America, can use their tails to cling onto branches as they swing from tree to tree.

A spider monkey swings through the rainforest looking for food and shelter.

QUIZ TIME!

Which of these big cats doesn't live in the rainforest?

a. jaguar

b. cheetah

c. puma

Answer on page 32.

In temperate rainforests, in places such as North America, animals like wolves and grizzly bears live on the forest floor. Animals such as squirrels and chipmunks spend a lot of time in the trees, along with many types of birds.

Animal and plant partners

Plants and animals need each other. When animals such as monkeys, insects and birds feed on **nectar** in flowers, they pick up **pollen**, which they carry to the next flower. This pollinates the flowers so they produce fruits and seeds. Many other animals need to eat flowers, fruits and seeds to survive.

Plants also help animal life cycles. Rainwater held in bromeliads provides a place for poison dart frogs to keep their tadpoles safe.

Leaf-tailed geckos are camouflaged to look like tree bark.

Defences

Some animals use camouflage to hide from predators or prey. Sloths curl their bodies up to look like part of a tree as they hang upside down from a branch. Their hair is covered in green **algae** so they are well hidden among the trees. **Reptiles**, such as geckos, are hard to see because they look like dried leaves or moss. Chameleons can change to be the same colour as leaves or branches. Poison dart frogs have colourful bright markings to warn predators that they are poisonous. Tropical fish such as angelfish, which live in the warm waters of the River Amazon, often have striped bodies. Black stripes on a colourful background help the fish to camouflage themselves among the plants.

Poison dart frogs use the water that collects in bromeliads to keep their tadpoles safe.

? What other animals do you think live in the rainforest? Turn the page to find out.

Rainforest birds

Birds are important to the rainforest. When they eat berries and fruits, the seeds inside pass through their bodies and come out in their poo. This spreads the seeds around the forest where they can grow into new trees. Many different kinds of birds live in temperate rainforests, including pheasants, nuthatches and flycatchers. Colourful birds including parrots and toucans live in the tropical rainforest canopy. They have long beaks with sharp edges for tearing and crushing fruits and berries. Toucans and a type of parrot called a macaw nest in holes in trees. They live mainly in the canopy. Hawks, owls and eagles hunt for smaller birds and animal prey, such as reptiles, fish and **rodents**.

Toucans have huge beaks. Some beaks are nearly half as long as the toucan's body!

HAVE A GO
Scatter some mixed wild bird seed in the garden to see what grows. The plants that grow will produce more seed for birds to find and eat.

Quick FACTS

• All kinds of animals from frogs, birds and lizards to elephants and tigers live in rainforests.
• Some animals can also help to spread plant species around the rainforest.

QUIZ TIME!

Why do you think toucans have colourful beaks?

  a. to warn other animals they are poisonous

  b. as camouflage from predators

  c. to attract a mate

Answer on page 32.

Make this

Rainforest rivers are home to lots of colourful fish such as the freshwater angelfish. Have a go making a shoal of these bright fish.

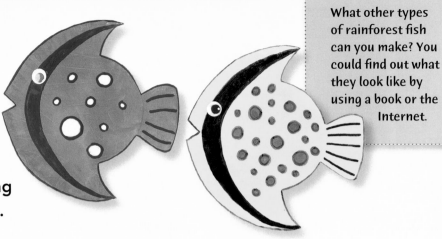

What other types of rainforest fish can you make? You could find out what they look like by using a book or the Internet.

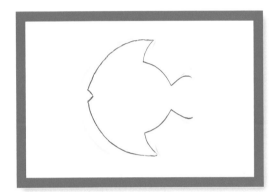

1 Cut a paper plate into a simple fish-shape, like the one shown.

2 Paint the plate in a bright colour and leave it to dry.

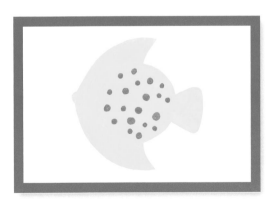

3 Paint colourful spots or scales on the body of your fish.

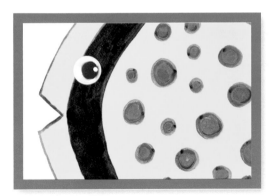

4 Use a felt-tip pen to draw thick stripes or other markings such as tail fins. Stick on a googly eye just above the mouth.

RAINFOREST PEOPLES

Tribal peoples have been living in the rainforests for thousands of years.

There are over a thousand different tribal peoples, mainly living in tropical rainforests around the world. Each tribe has its own way of life and language. They understand how important the rainforest is and care for it. They take only what they need for food, shelter and medicine so that they live in harmony with the trees or the animals that share the forest with them.

The Kayapo people live in the Amazon rainforest in Brazil.

QUIZ TIME!

Some rainforest peoples use poison from poison dart frogs for hunting.

Which of these is the most poisonous?

a. **golden dart frog**

b. **strawberry poison dart frog**

c. **bumblebee poison dart frog**

Answer on page 32.

Hunting and gathering

Rainforest peoples are skilled at hunting and tracking animals. They make their own hunting weapons such as spears for fishing and blowpipes that shoot poisonous darts. But they also use modern weapons, such as guns. They gather plants from the forest for food and medicine, but will also trade their goods with people from nearby towns and cities.

Yanomami hunters use spears, bows and blowpipes to hunt for their prey.

HAVE A GO
Try making a musical instrument using only natural materials, such as wood, bamboo, sticks, pebbles, nuts or coffee beans.

Rainforest children learn about forest foods and skills, such as hunting, from an early age.

Homes and communities

Some tribes move around the forest from place to place. Others live in one place and grow crops such as sweet potatoes. They use wood and plants from the forest to build their homes and make household items, crafts, hunting weapons and musical instruments. Some tribes live together in large homes around an area of land that they use for cooking, chores and ceremonies. In other tribes, men and women live apart. Children learn skills like hunting and tracking animals from their parents, families and other tribe members.

This Surui tribe member is wearing an elaborate tribal headdress made from feathers.

Under threat

Traditional ways of life of the rainforest peoples are under threat. In some places, outsiders have moved in and taken their land away. Some tribal peoples now only wear modern clothing and use modern tools and household items. New technology and contact with people from outside the forest can be good for tribal peoples, but their traditional skills and crafts could be lost if they give up the old ways of hunting, and living. Outsiders can also bring in new diseases that the rainforest people are not **immune** to.

Craftwork

Tribes have their own rich culture and art. Some tribes make craftwork to trade or sell to tourists. They are skilled at using materials including wood, plant fibres and feathers. Each tribe has its own way of making objects like masks and headdresses, which they also wear for dancing and ceremonies.

The Yanomami weave baskets – used for harvesting their crops – from strips of bark.

Make this

When tribal peoples celebrate their culture, they often wear amazing costumes, make-up and masks. You can make your own mask using card, paint, beads, feathers and scraps of fabric.

Perform a tribal rainforest dance wearing your mask. You could make a musical instrument to perform with, too!

1 Cut an oval shape from cardboard that will cover your face. Cut holes for your eyes and nose and a slot for your mouth. (Ask an adult to help you do this.)

2 Cut out shapes from coloured paper and stick them onto the front of your mask.

3 Add spots, stripes and other decorations with paints or felt-tip pens. Leave your mask to dry.

4 Stick on strips of raffia for hair. Tape string decorated with beads and feathers to the bottom of your mask. Punch a hole in each side of the mask. Then tie elastic to the holes to keep the mask in place on your face.

SAVING RAINFORESTS

It is important to protect rainforests as many are under threat.

Large areas of rainforest are being lost every year as trees are cut down and an area is cleared, sometimes by setting fire to the trees. Some experts think that we are losing over 325 square kilometres of tropical rainforest every day. The forest is cleared to make way for logging, mining, cattle ranching or farming and new roads are built to move goods and people around.

Huge areas of this rainforest in Sumatra, Indonesia have been cleared by burning down the trees.

Climate change

Climate change is also a threat to rainforests. Scientists think that the Earth's climate is warming up because carbon dioxide and other **greenhouse gases** trap heat. These gases are produced by industry and transport and lots of **methane** is produced by cows! Trees store carbon dioxide in their wood and leaves. They turn it back into oxygen, which they release back into the atmosphere. Smaller rainforests means there are fewer trees making oxygen. When trees are chopped or burned down, the carbon dioxide inside them goes back into the atmosphere.

Logging companies cut down lots of tropical trees that are made into furniture and other goods.

Animals and plants

Some rainforest animals, such as elephants, orang-utans, jaguars and tigers, are **endangered**. This means they are at risk of dying out because of hunting, **poaching** and deforestation. Many other animals that live in the rainforest are also in danger. As more forest habitat is destroyed, we may lose as many as 50,000 plant, animal and insect species. In some forests, dams have been built across rivers to provide power for electricity for towns and cities. This can harm fish and other wildlife living in and along the rivers. Rainforest animals, including reptiles, big cats and birds are also taken illegally for the **exotic** pet trade.

Orang-utans are threatened by the loss of their rainforest habitat.

QUIZ TIME!

How many football pitch-sized areas of rainforest are cut down every year?

a. **1 million**
b. **5.5 million**
c. **8.5 million**

Answer on page 32.

Quick *FACTS*
Threats to the rainforest and its animals are:
• Clearing trees for logging or farming.
• The exotic pet trade.

? Is there anything you can do to help save rainforests? Turn the page to find out.

Saving rainforests

What can you do?

We can all do something to help save the rainforests. We can try to raise money to help **conservation** organisations that work to protect the forests, their animals and peoples. We can find out more about rainforests and help other people understand how important they are. We can look for things that are sold under the Rainforest Alliance (above, right) or Fairtrade labels, because they mean that the people who grew or made them have been paid a fair price for their work, and the land and rainforests have been protected, too.

Recycling paper

Another way we can help temperate rainforests is to make sure we don't waste paper. Many trees are cut down illegally every year to make paper. Using recycled paper and taking care not to waste paper helps to save trees.

HAVE A GO
Cut out designs from used gift-wrap or cards to make your own gift tags. Make a hole in the top of each tag with a hole-punch and thread ribbon or tape through it.

Make this

SAVE THE RAINFOREST

You can help raise awareness about saving rainforests by decorating your own 'Save the Rainforest' T-shirt. You could make them for your friends and family, too.

What other messages about rainforests could your T-shirt carry? You could make a 'save the tiger' or 'save the orang-utan' T-shirt instead.

1 Before you start, make sure you get permission to use a T-shirt. Draw the shape of a rainforest animal on card, such as a frog. Ask an adult to cut out the middle of the animal shape to create a stencil.

2 Tape a stencil onto your T-shirt.

3 Dab fabric paint through the stencil onto the T-shirt. Leave to dry. Repeat with the stencil in a different place or with another stencil.

HINT: if you flip your stencil over you will get a mirror image of your original image.

4 Paint the words 'Save the Rainforest' onto the front of your T-shirt using fabric paint. Leave your T-shirt to dry.

GLOSSARY

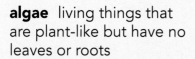

algae living things that are plant-like but have no leaves or roots

atmosphere a thin layer of gases covering a planet

bromeliads plants with a short stem and a rosette of stiff, shiny leaves

camouflage a way of hiding something so it looks like its surroundings

canopy something that forms a cover over an area

carbon dioxide a natural gas found in the atmosphere

carnivorous meat-eating

climate the usual weather conditions for a place

climate change the heating up or cooling down of Earth's atmosphere over a long period of time

conservation work done to protect and preserve

deciduous a type of tree or plant that loses its leaves each year

endangered an animal or plant that is in danger of dying out forever

Equator the imaginary line around the centre of the Earth

evergreen a type of tree or plant that keeps its leaves all year

exotic unusual or beautiful plants, animals or places

fungi a group of living things that includes mushrooms

greenhouse gases gases such as carbon dioxide that help trap heat in the Earth's atmosphere

habitat the natural home of an animal or plant

immune able to fight off a disease without medicine

mammals animals with hair that feed their young with the mother's milk

methane a natural gas

microbes tiny living things that can only be seen under a microscope

nectar sweet liquid that plants use to attract insects and birds

nutrients something in food that helps people, animals and plants live and grow

oxygen a natural gas found in the atmosphere

poaching illegally killing animals for their meat, fur, bones or ivory

polar the cold areas at the top and bottom of Earth

pollen tiny grains inside a flower that some plants use to reproduce

predators animals that hunt and eat other animals

prey animals that are hunted by other animals for food

recycle to break something down and turn it into something else

reproduce to make more of the same

reptiles a group of cold-blooded animals

rodents small mammals that have long front teeth

species a group of living things that share a name and can breed

spores tiny bodies that can grow into new plants

temperate a place with mild temperatures

tendril a thin shoot that plants use to help them cling onto things

tribal belonging to a group that shares the same ancestors, culture and beliefs

tropics the areas on Earth above and below the Equator

BOOKS

Eco Alert: Rainforests
by Rebecca Hunter (Franklin Watts , 2012)

Great Planet Earth: River Amazon
by Valerie Boden (Franklin Watts, 2014)

Espresso Ideas Box: Rainforests
by Deborah Chancellor (Franklin Watts, 2011)

Unstable Earth: What Happens if the Rainforests Disappear?
By Mary Colson (Wayland, 2014)

Up Close: Rainforest by Paul Harrison (Franklin Watts, 2011)

WEBSITES

kids.mongabay.com
A colourful website packed with facts on rainforests and the animals and peoples living in them.

www.msu.edu/user/urquhart/rainforest
The 'virtual rainforest' website, with pictures, videos, and lots of information about tropical rainforests.

www.rainforest-alliance.org/kids
The children's section of the website of the Rainforest Alliance, the organisation that runs a certification scheme for rainforest products, including facts, online games, activities and virtual rainforest visits.

NOTE TO PARENTS AND TEACHERS:
Every effort has been made by the Publishers to ensure that these websites are suitable for children, that they are of the highest educational value, and that they contain no inappropriate or offensive material. However, because of the nature of the Internet, it is impossible to guarantee that the contents of these sites will not be altered. We strongly advise that Internet access is supervised by a responsible adult.

INDEX

QUIZ ANSWERS

Page 4: a - the Amazon
Page 12: b - 45 metres
Page 18: b - cheetah
Page 20: c - to attract a mate
Page 22: a - golden dart frog
Page 27: c - 8.5 million